THE POPULAR HANDBOOK OF RARER BRITISH BIRDS

LIST OF ARTISTS

Coloured Plates

NORMAN ARLOTT
ROLAND GREEN
H. GRÖNVOLD
M. A. KOEKKOEK
G. E. LODGE
DAVID REID-HENRY
PHILIP RICKMAN
PETER SCOTT

Black-and-white Plate

P. J. HAYMAN

Text Drawings

ROBERT GILLMOR
P. J. HAYMAN

The Popular Handbook of Rarer British Birds

P. A. D. HOLLOM
Author of The Popular Handbook of British Birds, co-author of The Field Guide to the Birds of Britain and Europe, and an editor of The Birds of the Western Palearctic

H. F. & G. WITHERBY LTD
5, Plantain Place, Crosby Row, London, SE1 1YN

First published 1960
Reprinted 1966
Second edition (revised) 1980

ISBN 0 85493 129 5

PLATES PRINTED BY EBENEZER BAYLIS AND SON LTD.
AND YSEL PRESS, DEVENTER, HOLLAND

TEXT PRINTED IN GREAT BRITAIN BY
EBENEZER BAYLIS AND SON LTD,
THE TRINITY PRESS, WORCESTER, AND LONDON

INTRODUCTION

When *The Popular Handbook of British Birds* was being planned it was found impracticable to include all the species on the British list, and those which had occurred less than a dozen times had to be excluded. The present work is the fulfilment of hopes eventually to produce a companion volume dealing on similar lines with the remaining species, the rarities.

Generally speaking, then, the birds treated here have been recorded in Great Britain or Ireland on less than 12 occasions, but in a few cases additional records since 1950 have raised the number beyond this level, and for such species the occurrences have not been enumerated in detail. Quite exceptionally the Collared Dove, which was unknown here a decade ago, has invaded Britain from the continent and is now breeding in several counties.

This book, like *The Popular Handbook*, is based primarily on *The Handbook of British Birds*, and the debt owed to that work and all who contributed to it is enormous. Whilst the basic information on some species has remained virtually unchanged, many accounts have been augmented or modified to a greater or lesser degree, or almost entirely re-written to embrace new information which has become available in the post-war upsurge of ornithology. This increase in bird-watching and the establishment of bird-observatories have largely contributed to the addition of about 30 species which were not included in *The Handbook* of 1938–41.

One of the purposes of the present book is to provide British ornithologists with field descriptions and coloured plates of these new birds. David Reid-Henry has undertaken the exacting work of providing paintings of all these except for the Baikal Teal which Peter Scott very kindly painted for the book. The remaining colour plates and some line-drawings come from *The Handbook*, which source is gratefully acknowledged. I am very grateful also to Peter J. Hayman for the half-tone plate of Pratincoles and the line-drawings of Black Duck, wings of Pallid Harrier and Siberian Thrush, and heads of some American sandpipers; and to Robert Gillmor for drawings of Royal and Caspian Terns, and Collared and Turtle Doves.

In preparing the text many notes on field identification features have been taken from the pages of the journal *British Birds*, and I am also much indebted to the following who have willingly advised on the accounts of certain species or groups of species: H. G. Alexander, W. R. P. Bourne, D. D. Harber, P. J. Hayman, R. C. Homes, H. P. Medhurst, M. F. M. Meiklejohn, J. Paatela, J. Parslow, Roger T. Peterson, K. Williamson. The help given by I. J. Ferguson-Lees and I. C. T. Nisbet has been outstanding.

The formal acceptance of a new bird on to the British List calls for the investigation of many aspects and is often a protracted affair. The preparation of a book with specially painted coloured plates is also a lengthy task. Thus when the contents of this book were considered a year or more ago it was decided to make it as complete as possible with the inclusion of all valid records to the end of 1958 of all the rarer species which were expected to be on the British List in 1960. It was felt that readers would prefer the book to include one or two species not on the British List rather than omit any, and so some records have been retained although not yet adjudicated at the time of writing. The birds concerned are Baikal Teal, Western Sandpiper, Baltimore Oriole, and Summer Tanager, and in each case a footnote has been added to the text to show that official acceptance of these species on to the British List is as yet uncertain.

Thus the aim has been to include occurrences up to the end of 1958, and the main sources from which records have been taken are *The Handbook of British Birds* (Witherby *et al.*, 1938–1941), *The Birds of Scotland* (Baxter and Rintoul, 1953), *The Birds of Ireland* (Kennedy *et al.*, 1954) and the journals *British Birds*, *Scottish Naturalist*, *Scottish Birds* and *The Irish Bird Report*. Generally speaking records accepted by the authors and editors of these publications have been included without re-assessment, a major exception to this policy being the rejection of all the "Hastings records", i.e. the birds reputed to have been collected in the Hastings/Romney Marsh area between the years 1900 and 1916. The reasons why the exclusion of these records has been found necessary will be reviewed in *British Birds*.

The scientific nomenclature is based on publications of the British Ornithologists' Union. The English names are those in use in the journal *British Birds* with the following exceptions:

Pallas's Leaf Warbler is the name used for *Phylloscopus*

proregulus (generally known as Pallas's Warbler) to avoid confusion with Pallas's Grasshopper Warbler.

Citrine Wagtail (or Yellow-headed Wagtail) is the name given to *Motacilla citreola.* It has recently been added to the British List under the name of Yellow-headed Wagtail, but this can be a confusing choice as it seems to suggest that this distinct species is a race of the *flava* or *lutea* groups of the Yellow Wagtail which are known as Blue-headed, Grey-headed, Ashy-headed, etc. The bird is called Citron, or Citrine, Wagtail (in translation) in Czechoslovakia, Denmark, France, Germany, Holland and Spain.

Rufous Bush Robin is given as an alternative (following Vaurie in *The Birds of the Palearctic Fauna*) to the name of Rufous Warbler for *Agrobates galactotes,* to draw attention to the fact that it is more closely related to the chats than to the warblers.

P.A.D.H.
January 1960

NOTE TO SECOND EDITION

The first section of this book consists basically of a re-issue of the original text to the first edition. It omits, however, a few birds now discarded from the British list and, with the addition of a line or so at the end of the account of each species, gives the number of occurrences recorded during the period 1959–1978.

During this same period about 50 new species have been accepted as wild arrivals in Britain or Ireland, and the second section of the present edition contains descriptions and other details of these additional birds. Most of these have only been recorded since the first edition, but one or two result from older records which formerly were regarded as unacceptable; some adjustments have been necessitated by the ebbs and flows of taxonomic opinion on the validity of certain species. This new section is illustrated with plates (nos. 41–56) specially painted by Norman Arlott, whose knowledge of American birds as well as Old World species has been very helpful.

For technical reasons concerned with colour printing, it has not been feasible to amalgamate these additional plates with those published in the original edition. This influenced the decision to keep the new material in the form of a separate section following the original text, but a single index of course covers the whole of the present book, as does the table of contents (on pages 9–16) which includes details of order, family and genus. The Voous sequence has been adopted throughout.

In preparing the new text, the descriptions published in *British Birds* of rarities seen in this country have been freely consulted; I am grateful for information both published and unpublished from *Birds of the Western Palearctic* sources, and valuable help has been received from A. R. Kitson, R. Hudson, M. J. Rogers and Dr. J. T. R. Sharrock. The aim has been to include all records up to the end of 1978, and here the value of the work of the *British Birds* Rarities Committee and its annual reports is gratefully acknowledged; the difficulty of fulfilling such an aim without too long a delay is underlined by the omission of one or two occurrences such as that of the Belted Kingfisher. However, it is hoped that this book and the *Popular Handbook of British Birds*, taken together, now provide a useful combination of illustration and information on virtually all the species on the British and Irish lists.

P.A.D.H.
January, 1980

TABLE OF CONTENTS

PART ONE

Text: pages 17–144
Illustrations: plates 1–40 (between pp. 80 & 81)

Part One contains the species treated in the first edition, the number of occurrences being up-dated to the end of 1978.

WHITE-BILLED DIVER—*Gavia adamsii*

PLATE 1

Slightly larger than Great Northern Diver and distinguishable from it by the bill. This may range in *colour from whitish or ivory to straw-yellow,* darkening only at base particularly of the upper mandible to grey-brown or even bluish-green; the bill of the Great Northern Diver is blackish in summer, but in winter is largely pale grey and in young birds almost bluish-white especially at the base. Equally characteristic is the shape of the bill of White-billed Diver (see diagram below) having usually a practically straight upper mandible and with the lower mandible upward-angled for the greater part of its length, giving the *whole bill a marked up-tilted appearance*; the bill of the Great Northern Diver looks quite straight although the upper mandible is distinctly down-curved. In summer plumage the

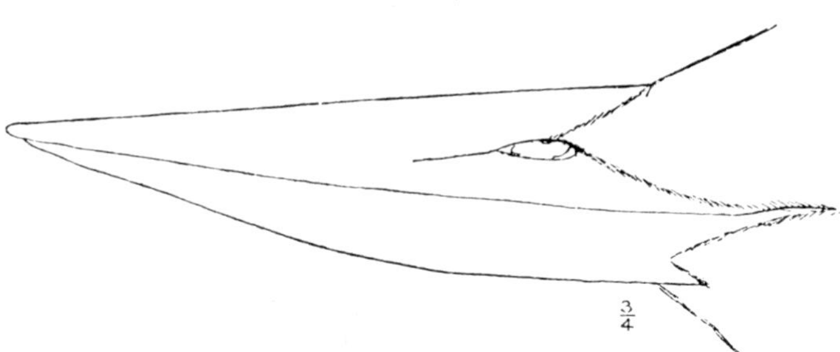

White-billed Northern Diver (*Gavia adamsii*), showing bill shape.

White-billed has the white spots on upper-parts, and especially on scapulars, larger than Great Northern's, and evidence of this feature is sometimes seen on winter visitors to British waters as the moult starts very early, sometimes in January. Additional features established by D. M. Burn and J. R. Mather include: Great Northern always has a dark ridge along top of bill from tip to base (White-billed never), White-billed typically holds bill pointing slightly upwards, enhancing uptilt effect, and in winter normally has more white on face embracing eye. Length up to about 33 ins. (84 cms.).

Habitat. Nearly all British records are from the coast or coastal inlets, but stragglers may appear on inland waters.

General Habits. Not known to differ from Great Northern Diver. It is apparently unable to fly when moulting its flight feathers, at least in early spring.

It is very seldom heard in winter quarters, but a captive bird occasionally called "gwook", short, liquid but muffled.

Food consists almost entirely of fish, with small quantities of crustacea, molluscs and worms.

Status and Distribution. Before 1946 only four British records. Dec. 1829, during 1830–32, spring 1852 and Feb–March 1916.

Since then there have been about fourteen occurrences. Nearly all have been on the east coast from Yorkshire northwards, with a concentration in Shetland; the dates cover all months from November to June.

The species breeds sporadically from the Murman coast along that of N. Siberia; it is less rare in N.E. Siberia. It also breeds in N. Alaska and Northwest Territories. It winters in Norwegian waters, also Bering Sea and Kuril Islands. There are no subspecies.

1959–1978 41 additional records

BLACK-BROWED ALBATROSS—*Diomedea melanophris*

PLATE 1

Albatrosses are distinguished from other sea-birds by their *large size, great span of narrow wings and gliding flight*, and are characteristic of the southern oceans. The body is stout, neck longer than in gulls, and the bill longer, heavier and hook-tipped. The Black-browed is the commonest of the albatrosses. It has the *upper surface of the wings and region of the back between them blackish, the rest of the head and body white*. It is the only white-headed albatross in which the adult has a *wholly yellow bill. This and the dark line over and through the eye* are diagnostic. The tail is black, the underside of wings white, but bordered with black, rather broadly in front and narrowly behind. Young birds resemble the adult, but crown and back of neck are suffused with slaty grey, under-surface of wings is mainly dark with pale central line, and bill is greyish black; later the head becomes white and the bill yellowish brown. Legs are usually greyish, darker blue or violet on joints and webs. Length about 31 ins. (79 cms.); maximum wing span about 8 ft. (2·45 m.).

There are no other albatrosses on the British List, but several other species have occurred as vagrants elsewhere in Europe, and must be taken into account in British identifications. The Yellow-nosed Albatross (*Diomedea chlororhynchos*) at all ages has a black bill (with yellow on tip and culmen when adult), much whiter pattern of underwing, and a distinct dark triangular patch in front of the eye nearly reaching the bill. The adult Grey-headed Albatross (*Diomedea chrysostoma*) is very similar to the Black-browed except in the usually bluish grey colour of the head; its bill is dark grey, with red tip and yellow markings. The Light-mantled Sooty Albatross (*Phoebetria palpebrata*), adult and immature, has a pearly body contrasting with dark cap and wings, and a conspicuous broken white eye-ring. The Wandering Albatross (*Diomedea exulans*), considerably larger with a wing-span of 11 ft., is mainly white when adult, with black wing-tips above and below; immature has same underwing as adult (thus lacking the black leading edge of Black-browed) and white face, forehead and throat, but is otherwise chocolate brown.

Habitat. Pelagic, coming to land to nest on islands.

General Habits. The general behaviour of all albatrosses is very similar. A large part of their life is spent in the air, gliding over the waves with wings held almost motionless. Only when the wind is fairly fresh can they continue their sailing flight for any length of time; when the wind drops they begin to flap their wings much more frequently. To obtain their food the birds come down gently on the water, usually with the wings raised. When settled with the wings closed they float very high. In order to take off again they begin by running along the surface with outstretched wings.

The bird is silent at sea away from breeding places, apart from a peevish croaking note when feeding.

Food. Cuttle-fish is included, as well as floating refuse from ships.

Status and Distribution. Great Britain—Two.

An exhausted bird picked up near Linton, Cambs., July 9, 1897.

Immature captured at Stavely, Derbys., a few days before August 21, 1952. (An albatross, believed to be this species, was seen off Fair Isle, Shetland, on May 14, 1949.)

The species breeds in southern seas from Cape Horn district, Falkland Is., Staten Is., S. Georgia and Prince Edward Is. to Campbell and Auckland Is. It occurs off the South African coast; occasionally in the North Atlantic north to Norway, Faeroes and Spitsbergen. There are no subspecies.

1959–1978 Some 20 additional records, most attributable to a bird summering in Scottish gannetries: Bass Rock 1967–69 and Unst 1974–78 (nest-building 1976)

CAPPED PETREL—*Pterodroma hasitata*

PLATE 1

A rather large petrel, bigger than Manx Shearwater. It resembles a Great Shearwater in appearance and flight, but is distinguished by the large *wedge-shaped area of white at the base of the tail*, *the white forehead and sides of the face* with a short, thick black bill and pure white under-parts; the white collar round back of neck does not darken on nape. The upper-parts are sooty brown, having a more or less greyish cast to the back and a dusky tinge along the sides. The under-surface of the wings is white, outlined in black, with the dark margin heavier in front; it is this white under-wing which best separates it from the non-British Soft-plumaged and Trinidade Petrels (*Pterodroma mollis* and *P. arminjoniana*). Length about 16 ins. (41 cms.).

Habitat. Pelagic, breeding in mountains of West Indian islands in or above the forest zone.

General Habits. Unlike the smaller petrels, it is said to pay no attention to the wake of a vessel, although at times it may approach close. It has a very fast gliding flight in great arcs close to the water, with quick bursts of flapping between each glide.

It has a mournful cry at breeding places.

Food includes fish.

Status and Distribution. England—One.

Caught on a heath near Swaffham, Norfolk, in March or April 1850.

Formerly bred freely on many islands of the West Indies; present status obscure but colonies of unknown size probably persist on Hispaniola and possibly elsewhere, especially Dominica.

1959–1978 No additional records

BULWER'S PETREL—*Bulweria bulwerii*

PLATE 2

A small, entirely dark petrel with long tail appearing square-ended, and short legs. It is smaller than any other dusky petrel, and slightly larger than any of the dark storm-petrels. The whole plumage is sooty-black, rather paler on the chin and edges of the greater wing-coverts; there is no white at the base of the tail. It is widely distributed over both the Atlantic and Pacific oceans but is rarely seen at sea. Bill is black; legs and part of webs very pale flesh, rest of webs dusky-black. Length about 10½ ins. (27 cms.).

Habitat. Pelagic, breeding on rocky islands.

General Habits. It is stated rarely to flock, and to be almost entirely nocturnal in habits. Breeding birds come to land as soon as it is dark, and leave as dawn approaches.

Call of incubating birds is a barking or frog-like "whok".

Food includes fish-eggs and crab-jelly.

Status and Distribution. England—Three.

One found dead Tanfield, Yorks., May 8, 1837.

One found dead near Beachy Head, Sussex, Feb. 3, 1903.

One found dead near Scarborough, Yorks., Feb. 28, 1908.

The species breeds in Atlantic in Azores, Madeiras, Salvages and Canaries; and in Pacific from Japan to Hawaii and Marquesas Is. There are no subspecies.

1959–1978 Two additional records. The Beachy Head record of 1903 is no longer accepted

LITTLE SHEARWATER—*Puffinus assimilis*

PLATE 2

The Little and Audubon's Shearwaters are very closely related species which replace each other in different zones of surface water at sea; intermediate populations occur at the North Atlantic islands which are probably indistinguishable in the field. Both species resemble the Manx Shearwater, but they are smaller, brown or black above and white beneath with more white in front of the eye, and proportionately shorter in the wing, flying with a *very rapid fluttering wing-beat between shorter spells of gliding*. In the southern hemisphere the Little Shearwater is typically jet black above with much white above and in front of the eye and on the lores and cheeks, with *pure white inner vanes to the primaries and undertail coverts*, and blue legs and feet; Audubon's Shearwater is rich dark brown above, with less white on the sides of the head, and brown inner vanes to the primaries and under-tail coverts, and flesh-coloured legs and feet. The Little Shearwaters of the Azores, Madeira, the Salvages, and Canaries are rather sooty above with dark tips to the under-tail coverts. The under-tail coverts, usually quoted as a good field character, are variable and difficult to see clearly, and the best character is probably the general colour of the upper-parts (sooty-black in Little, browner in Audubon's), and the relatively contrasting black and white appearance of the Little Shearwater in flight owing to the greater contrast in its markings, as opposed to Audubon's Shearwater, which appears to a larger extent dark with a white belly. Length about 11 ins. (28 cms.).

Habitat. Pelagic, but it seems ordinarily not to range so far as most shearwaters from its breeding islands.

General Habits. They are most often seen in scattered flocks or small parties within touch of the islands on which they breed, and generally resting on water, rarely alone far out at sea. When disturbed they fly away for some little distance with wings beating rapidly; the impression is given of great haste, but little speed. This description applies in calm waters near land, but in rougher weather flight is gliding, as in all shearwaters, but the wings are beaten much more often than in large shearwaters—four or five beats and then a short glide, and so on; flight is low. A surface feeder, but dives rather freely and sometimes for a long distance.

Cry resembles Manx Shearwater, but is said to be much feebler and higher in the case of the Madeiran race.

Food includes fish and cephalopods.

Status and Distribution. British Isles—Six.

One caught off Bull Rock, Co. Cork, May 6, 1853.

Male found dead near Earsham, Norfolk, about April 10, 1858.

Male picked up exhausted Welling, Kent, Aug. 20, 1912.

Female picked up dead Blakeney Point, Norfolk, May 11, 1929.

One seen Aberdaron, Caernarvons., May 7–9, 1951.

Female picked up dying near Stockport, Cheshire, May 10, 1958.

The race concerned, *Puffinus assimilis baroli*, breeds on Azores, Salvages, Madeira and Canaries. Other races occur in many parts of the southern hemisphere.

1959–1978 43 additional records

WHITE-FACED PETREL (or FRIGATE PETREL) —*Pelagodroma marina*

PLATE 2

It is distinguished from all other small petrels by *wholly white under-parts*, including under wing-coverts (but with darker flight and tail-feathers), and by conspicuously contrasted pattern. The crown and ear-coverts are slaty, darker than the back; it has a conspicuous white frontal band extending back to form a wide stripe above the eye; the general colour of the upper-parts is brownish-grey, with pale grey upper tail-coverts contrasted with blackish tail; the wing-quills are also blackish. The long legs are black, with webs orange, and extend a little beyond tail. Length about 8 ins. (20 cms.).

Habitat. Pelagic, resorting chiefly to turfy and sandy islands for breeding.

General Habits. Flight is exceedingly erratic. The long dangling legs are conspicuous during periods of pattering on water; when flitting overland to nesting grounds they just "tip" it with their toes, and bounce along, giving the impression of being full of springs; they have also been likened to "huge long-legged flies". Nocturnal at breeding colonies like most other petrels. When on the ground, owing to the extraordinary length of legs it is about the most awkward and helpless of all the small petrels. It does not normally feed in the wake of ships.

It is usually silent on the wing, but on breeding grounds has a faint note with a Redshank-like quality and on or below ground in breeding colony gives a mournful "wooo" which may be expanded into a siren-like moaning.

Food is small crustacea and probably other plankton organisms.

Status and Distribution. Great Britain—Two.

One picked up dead Walney Island, Lancs., Nov., 1890.

Young female caught alive Colonsay, Inner Hebrides, Jan. 1, 1897.

The race concerned, *Pelagodroma marina hypoleuca*, breeds on the Salvages and Cape Verde Islands. Other races occur in the Tristan da Cunha group, and in Australian and New Zealand seas.

1959–1978 No additional records. The Walney Island record of 1890 is no longer accepted

MADEIRAN PETREL—*Oceanodroma castro*

PLATE 3

Similar to the other small petrels and very difficult to identify in the field, but W. R. P. Bourne makes the following points. It more resembles Storm Petrel than Leach's Petrel; it has a characteristic fluttering flight rather like the Storm Petrel, but sometimes patters over the waves like Wilson's Petrel or swoops like Leach's Petrel; the white rump is more prominent and the legs more often seen than in Leach's, while wings seem longer and feet seen beyond the tail much less often than in Wilson's Petrel; noticeably larger and longer-winged than Storm Petrel, but otherwise similar; looks slightly browner than other small petrels; with experience the flight might prove the best character. The webs of feet are dark, but failure to see yellow webs does not necessarily mean a bird is not Wilson's Petrel as colour of Wilson's webs is very hard to see in field. In the hand it shows a slightly forked tail, pure white rump (lacking the inconspicuous smoky grey central dividing line of Leach's), and the upper tail-coverts forming the base of this white rump patch have prominent sharply defined black ends, but none of these features are of value in the field. Bill, legs and feet are black. Length about $7\frac{1}{2}$ ins. (19 cms.).

Habitat. Essentially a pelagic bird, resorting to islands for breeding.

General Habits. In habits it resembles Leach's Petrel. It is stated to follow in the wake of ships, which Leach's does not habitually do, but this requires confirmation. Like the other small petrels it is active at sea by day, but only comes to land at breeding haunts by night.

The typical note at the breeding site, uttered on the wing and in burrow, is a four- or five-syllabled squeak like the sound produced by a wet finger on a pane of glass.

Food. There is very little definite information.

Status and Distribution. British Isles—Two.

One picked up dead Milford, Hants., Nov. 19, 1911.

One Blackrock Lt., off Co. Mayo, Oct. 18, 1931.

The species breeds in the Atlantic on the Azores, Madeira, Salvages, Cape Verde Islands, St. Helena and Ascension; in Pacific in Galapagos, Hawaiian islands and islands off Japan. There are no subspecies.

1959–1978 No additional records

MAGNIFICENT FRIGATEBIRD—*Fregata magnificens*

PLATE 3

Frigatebirds are large tropical sea-birds with *long angled wings*, *long forked tails* and unparalleled powers of flight: effortless almost stationary floating on motionless wings, soaring, sailing, or cutting into the teeth of a gale. Their name is derived from their piratical feeding habits. The inner halves of their wings show a distinctive "hump" when soaring. Females are larger than males.

The Magnificent Frigatebird has a wing span of up to 8 ft. The plumage of the adult male is *entirely black with a purple sheen*, and at the chin an orange-red pouch of bare skin which in display may be greatly inflated like a balloon; the female has breast, upper belly and sides pure white and a whitish collar, the rest of the plumage being browner black than male, and with a paler bar running diagonally across the inner half of the upper wing to the carpal joint. Bill dark horn or bluish in male, horn in female; legs black in male, red in female. Young birds have head, neck and underparts white, often with a brownish extension from the sides forming a broken breast-band, but otherwise resemble female. Length about 40 ins. (102 cms.).

No other species of frigatebird is known with certainty to have visited Europe, but three others breed in tropical South Atlantic, and may be separated from Magnificent Frigatebird as follows: Great Frigatebird (*Fregata minor*) male has brown band across inner half of upper wing but is otherwise indistinguishable, female has whitish (not black) throat, young have the white parts tinged rusty. Ascension Frigatebird (*Fregata aquila*) male and female are both all-black when adult and indistinguishable from male Magnificent on the wing, juveniles at first almost inseparable but later breast darkens, leaving only head white. Lesser Frigatebird (*Fregata ariel*) adult male has a conspicuous white patch on sides of body under the wing unlike any other frigatebird, female has dirty white throat like Great Frigatebird but also has chestnut collar on hind neck, young have white parts streaked rusty and the head sometimes brown.

Habitat. Exclusively aerial by day, haunting tropical coastal waters and sometimes soaring over land. They breed on islands and roost on trees.

General Habits. When not breeding it spends the whole day in the air, never diving nor settling on water or land, and cannot really walk or swim, the feathers being non-water-repellent to an unusual degree. Food is taken on the wing, largely from the surface of the sea, the bird being said often to swoop from a great height, striking downward with the beak into the sea, making a sound like the hiss of an arrow shot into the water, and then, without wetting feathers or feet, rising and dexterously tossing up the prey before swallowing it; food is also obtained in the air skua-wise from other sea-birds which are forced to disgorge by a close and agile pursuit and if necessary a vicious peck. Gregarious, particularly when nesting and roosting.

Frigatebirds are usually silent.

Food is largely fish, often good-sized, also jelly-fish and other animal matter including offal.

Status and Distribution. Scotland—One.

An immature female caught in an exhausted condition Tiree, Inner Hebrides, July 9, 1953.

The Scottish bird belonged to the race *Fregata magnificens rothschildi* which breeds from the Caribbean south to Brazil, and in the Pacific from Mexico to Ecuador. Other races occur in Galapagos and Cape Verde islands. The bird ranges north to Florida and very rarely to E. Canada, and in Europe two frigatebirds, both probably of this species, have been taken in France.

1959–1978 No additional firm records

CATTLE EGRET—*Bubulcus ibis*

PLATE 4

A small white heron with a tuft of *pale buffish feathers on the crown* in winter; in summer the crown is rather darker and the *mantle and breast are buff* also, but even in summer the pale buff plumes are inconspicuous at a little distance. Hence it can be confused on the ground with Little Egret, and in the air with Squacco also, mixed flights not being infrequent in areas where the three species are present. When perched it can be separated from Little Egret by its slightly shorter length which is accentuated by its *stockier build and thicker neck*; and by usually yellow bill (Little Egret's is black) and *heavy jowl protruding under the bill*, these last two features being discernible in flight too, and then serving also as a distinction from the smaller Squacco. The legs of the Cattle Egret become red at the height of the mating season but are otherwise mainly yellow in summer, becoming drabber and darker in winter (Little Egret's are always black with yellow feet); the bill reddens at the same time as the legs. Habitual association with cattle in fields is highly characteristic, Little Egret preferring wetter places. Total length about 20 ins. (51 cms.); body about 11 ins. (28 cms.).

Habitat. Often resorts to marshes or water-side for breeding, but is otherwise much less aquatic than other herons, frequenting indifferently dry grasslands or marshes wherever there are cattle, and also feeding on arable land.

General Habits. Very sociable, nearly always in flocks or parties, and feeds especially among grazing cattle. In flights, roosts and breeding colonies it often mixes with other species such as Little Egret. Flight is leisurely and the wings rather rounded.

At breeding places birds have various croaking notes.

Food is largely insects disturbed by grazing cattle; also frogs and lizards.

Status and Distribution. England—Two.

Immature female near Kingsbridge, Devon, Oct., 1805.

Male shot Breydon Marshes, Norfolk, Oct. 23, 1917.

The race concerned, *Bubulcus ibis ibis*, breeds in Spain, Portugal (recently S. France), Africa, Madagascar and W. Asia; since 1930 it has colonized America from Brazil to U.S.A. Another race breeds in S. Asia from India eastwards, and in N. Australia.

1959–1978 17 additional records

GREAT WHITE EGRET—*Egretta alba*

PLATE 4

This species and Little Egret are the only herons with *pure white plumage*, although Cattle Egret has very little buff in winter and Squacco Heron looks mainly white in flight. At some distance in a swamp with nothing available for comparison, confusion with Little Egret is perfectly possible, but Great White Egret is actually *much bigger as well as proportionately slimmer* and more scrawny and kink-necked. It also looks slimmer and narrower-winged in flight apart from the size difference. Other differences from Little Egret are: absence of long crest, *feet blackish* instead of yellow, legs yellowish at sides and black in front; the *bill outside the breeding season is yellow*, but in the breeding season is largely black although yellow is retained at the base and sometimes more extensively. Cattle Egret also has a yellow bill for most of the year but is much stockier and thicker-necked and its heavy jowl is noticeable even in flight. It should be borne in mind that albinistic common Herons are seen from time to time and have been confused with Great White Egret. Total length about 35 ins. (89 cms.); body about 15 ins. (38 cms.).

Habitat. Frequents reedy swamps, meres, river-banks, deltas, nesting in dense reed-beds, but when not breeding can accept bare shores and mud-banks far from reeds.

General Habits. It feeds freely on the borders of open water like Grey Heron, and although mainly found in reedy localities it is not an essentially reed-haunting bird like Bittern or even Purple Heron. The European race appears rarely to perch in trees. It sometimes occurs singly, but more often in parties or flocks; it does not associate much with other species.

A very silent bird, but at times gives a harsh "graaar".

Food. Mainly fish, aquatic insects, frogs, etc., but in dry season takes mice, voles, land insects, lizards.

Status and Distribution. Great Britain—About ten.

Three Yorks. (1825, 1834, 1868).

One Notts., prior to 1838.

One E. Lothian, June, 1840.

One Cambs., May or June, 1849.

One Perths., May, 1887.

One seen Helston, Cornwall, Sept. 28–Oct. 20th, 1948.

One seen Gurthean, Cornwall, May 29, 1951.

One seen Wareham, Dorset, August 5, 1951.

The race concerned, *Egretta alba alba*, breeds in Europe eastwards from Czechoslovakia and Austria, across central Asia to Japan, and winters in Africa and S.W. Asia. Other races occur in Africa, India, S. Japan southwards to Australia and New Zealand, also America.

1959–1978 Seven additional records

RED-BREASTED GOOSE—*Branta ruficollis*

PLATE 5

The striking and *curiously formal colour-pattern of black, white and chestnut-red* renders the Red-breasted Goose unmistakable. Viewed from behind, the black crown and back of neck, upperparts and tail, with white rump, give an appearance not unlike Brent Goose; but in side view the bird has the side of the head white, with a vertical black line from crown to chin passing through the eye, and a patch on the ear-coverts chestnut-red. The whole of the front of neck and the upper breast are also chestnut-red and also have sharply defined white borders. The narrow white band round the base of the neck and across the breast, separating the red from the black of the lower breast, can in some lights be more noticeable than the red breast itself, while at a distance the white flank-stripe is the best field character. Bill and legs blackish, the bill very small and delicate. Young birds are duller. Length about 21–22 ins. (55 cms.).

Habitat. Outside the breeding season frequents mainly grasslands and crops in steppe-country, roosting on sandbanks or islands. Breeds chiefly on arctic cliffs.

General Habits. Are much like grey geese, and it often associates with Lesser White-fronted Geese. All movements are very quick and the head moves astoundingly fast in plucking grass.

Call is a double staccato screech, "kee-kwa" or "ee-e". There are always two syllables which are completely disjointed: the second sounds as though it is a strain on the voice, as the note seems a little broken.

Food. Green food is always necessary, and apparently it normally grazes almost exclusively on young shoots of grass.

Status and Distribution. Great Britain—There are now some 16 records, of which five have occurred between 1950 and 1958. Two records are from Wales and one Beauly Firth, N.E. Scotland, but majority are English from Northumberland south to Sussex, also Devon and several Gloucester. Dates extend from early October to early March, but most are in winter.

The species breeds in arctic Siberia, and winters mainly in the S. Caspian area, with small numbers in N. Greece and some reaching Hungary. There are no subspecies.

1959–1978 Nine additional records

BAIKAL TEAL—*Anas formosa*

PLATE 5

Appreciably larger than common Teal. The drake is most distinctive, appearing in spring to have a largely whitish head (browner earlier in the season). The main colour of side of head and neck is pale creamy buff, with a metallic green crescent extending from the eye towards the back of the head and down the side of the neck. The crown, hind neck and chin are black, and a narrow black bar from eye to chin runs more or less vertically down across the buffish cheek. The long drooping scapulars are black, white and rufous; the wing brown with mainly green speculum. The back and flanks are grey, the latter separated at the forward end by a white bar from the vinaceous-washed black spotted upper breast, and at the rear end by another white bar from the mainly black under-tail coverts. Rest of under-parts are white. The female is brown, not unlike common Teal but is readily distinguished by a *well-defined buffish white round spot on each side of the base of the bill*. The male in eclipse is much like female. Bill bluish grey, the relatively long legs grey. Total length about 16 ins. (41 cms.).

Habitat. Mainly a freshwater duck, but is also found on sea at times. They seem to feed fairly often on dry land, and on grain fields in winter.

General Habits. Its habits are said to resemble those of common Teal, and it is equally wary, although flight is not so swift or erratic. Gregarious outside breeding season, many thousands collecting together on passage or in winter quarters.

It is much more noisy than Teal. The note of the male is an un-ducklike deep chuckling "wot-wot" or "proop" which carries a considerable distance. The female has a Teal-like quack.

Food is mainly vegetable matter including rice and grain, but some insects and other animal food also taken.

Status and Distribution. Scotland—Two.

Female seen Fair Isle, Shetland, Sept. 30–Oct. 1, 1954.

Female shot Loch Spynie, Elgin, Feb. 5, 1958.

The species breeds in central and E. Siberia, and winters mainly in Japan and E. China. There are no subspecies.

1959–1978 Two additional records.

BLACK DUCK—*Anas rubripes*

PLATE 6

It is of Mallard size and shape, but the body plumage of both upper- and *under-parts is sooty brown*, considerably darker than female Mallard. The under-wing is silvery white (like Mallard's), providing in flight a *gleaming contrast with the dark body*, which is an immediately striking and distinctive character. The effect is black and white. Other features are that the rich purple speculum is not bordered in front with white, and there is *no white in tail* (which is so characteristic a feature of a female Mallard, Shoveler or Pintail flushing ahead of the observer). The sexes are similar. On the water the bird looks large and sooty, but the head and neck are paler, being buff with dark streaks, and with dark line through the eye and a narrow dark crown. At close range the pale edgings to the brown body feathers are evident enough, but at a distance it has been confused with Common Scoter which, however, has a stouter head, shorter neck, pointed tail, and other differences. Bill is olive or yellow, unmarked. Legs brown, orange or coral red, the adult male in full plumage having the brightest colours. Hybrids with Mallard are not infrequent. Total length about 23 ins. (58 cms.).

Habitat. It frequents much the same wide range of waters as Mallard: inland pools, streams and marshes, salt-marsh, and

on the sea itself especially when inland waters are frozen; likewise it is often found on lakes in city parks. Grain fields and wood edges with acorns and beechmast are at times visited for feeding.

General Habits. Like Mallard, flight is swift, with wings on the downward beat not coming much below the level of the body; when flushed it jumps nearly vertically 8 or 10 ft. off land or water. It walks easily, running if necessary, and swims lightly and gracefully. It does not normally dive but up-ends readily. Gregarious, but does not form very large flocks. In winter it feeds on marshes, etc., by night, resting by day on open water, ice or sand-bars, etc.

The female has a loud quack like female Mallard, and the male a more subdued "quek".

Food is mainly vegetable. Animal matter includes molluscs, crustacea, ants, insects and fish.

Status and Distribution. Ireland—One.

Adult female shot Listrolin, Kilkenny, a few days before Feb. 5, 1954.

The species breeds in N. America from Northern Manitoba to Labrador and Newfoundland and south to N. Carolina and west to the Great Lakes; it winters from S.E. Canada south to the Gulf of Mexico. There are no subspecies.

1959–1978 Seven additional records

BLUE-WINGED TEAL—*Anas discors*

PLATE 6

It is the size of a Garganey. Male is distinguished by dark grey-brown head with a *white crescent in front of the eye*. Back is red-brown with black and buff markings. *Under-tail coverts are black, bordered in front by a conspicuous white patch.* The speculum in the drake is metallic green with a white band in front, but in the female is much duller, with the bar buffish and inconspicuous; the *fore-wing is bright pale blue* (the same colour as in Shoveler, not blue-grey like Garganey). The female is much like duck Garganey, but with the blue of the fore-wing only a little duller than in drake and hence easily identified. Eclipse plumage begins in July, is complete in August and, as in Garganey, is long retained by adults; full plumage is seldom acquired before mid-winter and sometimes not until March. Bill of male is black, of female dusky with paler base and yellowish edges to both mandibles; legs of both sexes dull yellowish. Total length about 15 ins. (38 cms.), body about 10½ ins. (27 cms.).

(The Cinnamon Teal (*Anas cyanoptera*), native to western N. America, is another blue-winged duck. It is not on the British list, but is regularly kept as an ornamental waterfowl and breeds readily. The female is indistinguishable in the field from the duck Blue-winged Teal, although sometimes tending to be more reddish on the underparts; in the hand, her bill is usually larger (39·45 mm.) than that of duck Blue-winged Teal (38·40 mm.). The male in full plumage is very distinctive with head, neck and most of body feathers uniform rich cinnamon red.)

Habitat. In the breeding season it mainly frequents quite small ponds in a wide variety of country, but also larger fresh waters. In winter-quarters it chiefly haunts rice-fields and extensive marshes, but is fond of quite small pools and ditches.

General Habits. It is the American counterpart of the Garganey. Flight is swift. It perches freely on logs in flooded places. It feeds mainly on the surface, but sometimes "up-ends". Often very tame where not persecuted.

The male gives a high-pitched sort of squeak; the duck's note is a faint quack.

Food includes molluscs, insects and crustaceans; large quantities of vegetable matter comprising sedges, pondweeds, grasses and algae are also taken.

Status and Distribution. British Isles—About nineteen. Nearly half of these have occurred widely scattered in Ireland, others in Outer Hebrides, S. Scotland, Wales, W. and E. coasts of England. More females recorded than males. Found most frequently in autumn (especially September) and winter.

The species breeds across Canada (from N.W. to S.E.) and south over much of U.S.A. It winters from south U.S.A. south to Brazil and Ecuador. There are no subspecies.

1959–1978 52 additional records

RING-NECKED DUCK—*Aythya collaris*

PLATE 7

The Ring-necked Duck is the N. American counterpart of the Tufted Duck and, having a generally similar pattern of black and white plumage, could easily be passed over as being that species. The distinguishing features of the drake Ring-necked are: the *high dome set far back on the crown* and the steep, almost flat, even concave, back of the head; the slightly up-curved bill is dark grey-blue with a *noticeable clear-cut whitish ring* immediately short of the black tip, and has another narrow whitish band round the base, resulting in a *strongly pied pattern to the bill*; the large pale flank patch is not altogether pure white as in Tufted Duck, being delicately vermiculated pale grey except towards the front where the *white forms a crescent running up between the bend of the wing and the neck*, a conspicuous feature even at long range; an indistinct and inconspicuous chestnut collar rings the base of the neck; otherwise the head, neck, breast and back are black. The duck is best identified by her head-shape and bill-pattern, the same as in the drake; in addition she is a little paler and greyer plumaged than duck Tufted; has a narrow whitish eye-ring and whitish line running back from eye over the ear-coverts; a whitish area round base of bill, not so clean or sharply defined as Scaup's but extending farther onto lower cheeks and chin. In flight the broad pale wing-bar of both sexes is grey like Pochard's (not white like Tufted). Eye of male is orange-yellow, of female yellowish brown. Total length about 17 ins. (43 cms.), body about 11 ins. (28 cms.).

Habitat. It is essentially a freshwater duck, preferring marshes and shallow scrub-enclosed pools to bare open waters or rivers.

General Habits. An alert bird and excellent diver, obtaining much of its food underwater, but also dabbles around margins. It swims lightly and rises from the water with greater ease than most diving ducks. Moves usually in small flocks, or in ones and twos.

The call is deep and hoarse like other diving ducks, but is not often heard.

Food in winter is largely vegetable matter and includes water lilies, pondweeds, sedges and grasses; insects, molluscs, small frogs and fish are also taken.

Status and Distribution. England—One.

Male seen Slimbridge, Glos., March 12-14, 1955. (A male exposed for sale in Leadenhall Market, London, in January, 1801, was said to have been taken in the fens of Lincolnshire.)

The species breeds in U.S.A. from southwest to northeast, and north to central Canada. The winter range extends to Panama, but the bulk of population winters in U.S.A. in south-east states and those west of Rockies. There are no subspecies.

1959–1978 60 additional records

STELLER'S EIDER—*Polysticta stelleri*

PLATE 7

The black and white pattern of the drake, with *white head, dark (greenish) patch on nape, black collar round neck, and chestnut-buff breast and belly* shading to paler on flanks, is quite distinctive. As seen at rest the whole hind part of the body and wings are black with crescentic white mark on the wings; the long curving scapulars are banded lengthwise black and white. The centre of the back and the throat are also black. The rather long and pointed tail is usually inclined upwards at a moderate angle. It is a neat, compact-looking little duck, very different in build and outline from the heavy and coarse-looking Eider. In flight the white fore-wing is conspicuous. In the case of the female the question of confusion with the true eiders hardly arises, as apart from the *much smaller size and darker, more uniform colouring, the profile of the head and bill is quite different and more like a typical duck.* Her head is slightly paler than rest of plumage and more inclined to rufous; a white wing-bar is fairly prominent, with another less distinct in front of it, and the purple speculum between them may be visible as such in good light. Eclipse is assumed rather late in the summer, the male becoming much like female apart from the wings. Young birds are much like females, and during their first winter and spring the males make very incomplete approach to mature plumage. Bill and legs of adult male are bluish-grey, duller in female. Total length about 18 ins. (46 cms.); body about 12 ins. (30–31 cms.).

Habitat. It breeds on tundra, and non-breeding parties may frequent arctic coasts. In winter it tends to keep well out to sea in rough, deep rocky waters off ice-bound shores.

General Habits. Most observers have found the bird wild and shy, but some in both summer and winter have commented on its tameness. Flight is much swifter than that of other eiders, with whistling sound like Goldeneye's, but very much louder; it rises as easily as a surface-feeding duck. It feeds by day, partially opening wings when diving, and in shallows will "up-end" like a surface-feeder.

Note of female is a "growling" like female Wigeon's; male's is a low croon.

Food is almost entirely animal matter and includes molluscs, young fish, spawn and worms.

Status and Distribution. Great Britain—Five.

Nearly adult male Caistor, Norfolk, Feb. 10, 1830.

Young male off Filey Brigg, Yorks., Aug. 15, 1845.

Two seen (one of them a male) off Gairsay, Orkney, Jan. 5–19, 1947.

Male seen Deerness, Orkney, Jan. 13, 1949.

The species breeds in arctic Siberia and Alaska; in Europe it may nest irregularly in N. Norway where it has often summered. Winters on coasts of N. Scandinavia and N. Pacific. There are no subspecies.

1959–1978 Eight additional records

HARLEQUIN DUCK—*Histrionicus histrionicus*

PLATE 7

The drake is easily identified, having ground colour slaty-blue (looking black at distance), with *chestnut flanks and vivid white streaks on neck and breast* and a roughly triangular white patch occupying nearly the whole side of face between eye and bill. These white areas show conspicuously even in a poor light. It also has scapulars partly white, a metallic purple speculum, the inner secondaries mostly white, and a short white wing-bar.

The duck is uniform dull brown above and below, with a dull whitish breast *mottled with dark feathers* and, unlike female Bufflehead, has two white spots in front of eye, also the white spot behind the eye is round, not elongated. Moreover the female Harlequin is a larger and much darker bird, the shade of brown rather suggesting a female Scoter or young Long-tailed Duck; and the latter is the most likely bird to be confused with female Harlequin, since at a distance the detail of the Harlequin's two light spots becomes dim and both give the effect of light sides of head. The light belly of the Long-tail, if it can be seen, is then a valid distinction; the Bufflehead's belly is also white. Further points are: extreme buoyancy, habit of keeping apart from other species, and—most characteristic—the manner of swimming, either so closely abreast that the flank of each individual touches that of its neighbour or in step-like formation. Full plumage of male is complete from October to July; eclipse is not complete until the end of August when bird is dull slaty above, blacker below than female but with more white on face. Bill of adults is lead-blue with paler tip, duller in female; legs bluish. Total length about 17 ins. (43 cms.); body about 11½ ins. (29 cms.).

Habitat. In the breeding season it resorts to swift rivers. In winter it frequents coasts, but unlike other diving ducks prefers the roughest, rockiest shores of headlands and outer islands where the surf breaks over hidden ledges.

General Habits. Flight is rapid, swinging from side to side even more frequently than Long-tailed Duck. Walks with ease on rocks, etc. Sits high on the water and has a habit of jerking the head backwards and forwards at each stroke of the legs. Flocks are small and very compact. It is almost entirely a day-feeder. Frequently dives from the wing.

Food includes insects, small crustacea, molluscs, also worms and fish-spawn.

Status and Distribution. Great Britain—Seven.

Male found dead Filey, Yorks., autumn 1862.

Two young males obtained Farne Is., Northumberland, Dec. 2, 1886; adult male Farne Is. not long after.

Adult male shot mouth of R. Ribble, Lancs., winter 1914–15 or 1915–16.

Male seen Sound of Harris, Outer Hebrides, Feb. 13, 1931.

Young male shot on R. Teviot, Roxburgh, Jan. 16, 1954.

The race concerned, *Histrionicus histrionicus histrionicus*, breeds in Iceland (resident), Greenland and N.E. Canada; the latter birds winter south to Maine. Another race breeds E. Siberia to Alaska and south to California.

1959–1978 One additional record of a pair

BUFFLEHEAD—*Bucephala albeola*

PLATE 8

General plumage pattern recalls Goldeneye, but the bird is *considerably smaller* (being little larger than a Teal) and at once distinguished by *a broad white patch behind the eye in both sexes*, instead of (smaller) patch in front of the eye in drake only. In the drake it extends from eye to nape; in the duck it is smaller and less prominent. Moreover the duck seldom shows white on the closed wing, unlike the resting Goldeneye which has a white bar on the edge of wing. The duck Bufflehead might then, without aid of glasses, be mistaken for female Harlequin or possibly female Long-tailed Duck; Harlequin, however, has two white patches in front of the eye and the one behind is not so elongated, whilst female Long-tail looks much larger and appears whiter at all seasons, and unlike Bufflehead neither species has any white in the wing in flight. In flight the neck does not appear short, as in Goldeneye. Full plumage of adult male appears to be acquired about mid-October. Bill is bluish in male, dark lead-colour in female; legs of male are pinkish or coral, of female purplish grey. Total length about 15 ins. (38 cms.); body about 10 ins. (25 cms.).

Habitat. Outside the breeding season it occurs chiefly on coastal bays and estuaries, also regularly on larger open fresh waters. Nests near water in wooded country.

General Habits. A hardy, vivacious little duck. Like Goldeneye it is restless and much on the wing, seldom forming large flocks or consorting with other species. It rises from the water more easily and directly than most other diving ducks, and sometimes from below the surface; it usually flies low.

Notes are like feeble versions of Goldeneye's, but are seldom heard.

Food is chiefly animal matter, including fish, molluscs, shrimps, worms and insects. Some vegetable matter is also taken.

Status and Distribution. Great Britain—Five.
Adult male Yarmouth, Norfolk, about 1830.
One Bridlington, Yorks., winter 1864–5.
Adult male shot S. Uist, Outer Hebrides, June 1870.
Female, Tresco, Scilly Isles, Jan. 17, 1920.
Female seen several times off Hunstanton, Norfolk, Feb. 1932.

An American species breeding from Ontario across Canada to Alaska and south to California; it winters over much of U.S.A. south to Mexico and on Pacific coast north to Aleutian Is. There are no subspecies.

1959–1978 One additional record

HOODED MERGANSER—*Mergus cucullatus*

Plate 8

It is only slightly larger than Smew. The male is black and white; neck and head black with a *fan-shaped white crest* having a black border; breast white with two black bars in front of the wing, the wing dark with a small white patch on the hinder part; flanks brownish. Female is recognized as a merganser when close at hand by the narrow spike-like bill, and in flight by the long-drawn appearance of the bird with bill, neck, head and body held in a horizontal straight line; it is distinguished from females of Goosander and Red-breasted Merganser by the *small size*, *dark coloration*, *dark head and neck*, and bushy buffish crest; the wing is much like male's but with still less white on the trailing edge. Full plumage of adult drake is usually complete in October, young males not acquiring it before the middle of their second winter and until then much resembling females; in eclipse plumage in summer the male's head and neck become mottled brownish, and breast and flanks like those of female. Bill black, edged orange in female; legs of male yellowish-brown, of female more dusky. Total length about 18 ins. (46 cms.); body about 12 ins. (30–31 cms.).

Habitat. In the breeding season it resorts to quiet wooded lakes, pools and slow streams; at other seasons it frequents similar haunts as well as creeks and ponds of large marshes, retiring to swifter streams when other places are frozen. It very rarely occurs on salt water.

General Habits. Flight is extremely rapid with very quick wing-beats, sometimes with sharp and abrupt changes of direction; it is often on the wing, the male flying with the striking white crest depressed. On the water the crest may often be depressed and is then inconspicuous. The bird swims lightly, but sinks low in water when alarmed. Most dives appear to be short, the bird feeding a great deal in shallow water. It is mainly if not entirely diurnal, and rarely associates with other species. Shy and retiring. A very silent bird, but low croaking notes are heard in autumn.

Food is mainly animal matter, largely insects and fish, also crayfish, water-snails, frogs, etc. Some vegetable food is also taken: seeds, grain and aquatic plants.

Status and Distribution. British Isles—Six.

Young male Menai Strait, N. Wales, winter 1830–1.

A pair Cobh Harbour, Cork, Dec. 1878.

Female Shannon Estuary, Kerry, Jan. 1881.

Adult male shot Yell, Shetland, July 1884.

Female or immature seen Acton Lake, Armagh, Dec. 21, 1957.

An American species breeding from Alaska, central and S.E. Canada south to central U.S.A., and wintering from S.W. Canada to Florida and Mexico. There are no subspecies.

1959–1978 No additional records. The Yell record of 1884 is no longer accepted

BLACK KITE—*Milvus migrans*

PLATE 9

It is *darker, dingier-looking* and has a coarser, shaggier appearance than the Kite, and the *tail is much shorter and less deeply forked,* appearing almost straight-edged when expanded. Young birds have a pale patch on the under-wing recalling that of Kite, though smaller and much fainter, but in adults this is absent or much obscured. Upper-parts are very dark brown and under-parts rufous brown, some a good deal darker than others. Head is paler, usually looking more or less greyish brown in the field, but by no means so pale or so clearly differentiated from the body as in Kite. Young birds are paler with less uniform upper-parts (owing to pale tips to feathers), making more contrast between the quills and the rest of wing. If the forked tail is not seen or is expanded, the bird can be confused in flight with the dullest examples of Marsh Harrier which are rather similar in size, proportions and coloration; but the Black Kite's head is generally greyer, and it usually holds its wings level in gliding, when the Harrier's are raised to form a shallow "V". Bill is horn-black, legs orange-yellow. The two sexes are much the same size. Length about 22 ins. (56 cms.).

Habitat. In the breeding season it occurs largely in cultivated country in the neighbourhood of woods, especially near water, but it also commonly frequents uncultivated districts with scattered trees and may be regularly found hunting over more barren areas. In the east of its range it haunts towns as a scavenger.

General Habits. It is frequently seen flying or wheeling over water where it will pick up floating refuse and fish. It also takes prey from the ground much as Kite, but is more of a scavenger where it has the opportunity; and it is readily attracted by rubbish dumps; it will also frequent the breeding-places of herons, cormorants, etc., to obtain fish remains and other carrion. Insects are hawked in the air. Although isolated pairs occur, it is normally sociable.

Much more noisy than Kite, in the breeding season it has a peculiar half whinnying, half squealing cry not unlike the young of one of the larger gulls. It also calls, though less frequently, at other seasons.

Food in some areas is largely fish, also garbage and carrion. Other items are mammals to size of rabbit, birds, reptiles (snakes, lizards, frogs, toads, newts), insects, molluscs and worms.

Status and Distribution. Great Britain—Five.

Adult male Alnwick, Northumberland, May 11, 1866.

Male Aberdeen, April 16 or 18, 1901.

Juvenile Tresco, Scilly Isles, seen Sept. 6 and shot Sept. 16, 1938.

One seen Tresco, May 28–30, 1942.

Male shot Beal, Northumberland, May 14, 1947.

The race concerned, *Milvus migrans migrans*, breeds in S., central and E. Europe, W. Asia and N. Africa; it winters chiefly in tropical Africa. Other races occur in other parts of Africa, Australia, S. and S.W. Asia, and from E. Russia to Japan.

1959–1978 25 additional records

EGYPTIAN VULTURE—*Neophron percnopterus*

PLATE 9

The bold contrast of the *white plumage and black quills* of the adult precludes confusion with any other bird of prey, except perhaps momentarily with the under-side pattern of a pale-phase adult Booted Eagle (*Hieraaetus pennatus*) which is however a smaller Buzzard-shaped bird and has not occurred in the British Isles. At long range the Vulture can quite easily be confused with White Stork until the latter's long neck and legs both extended in flight are distinguished. Immature birds are dark brown mottled buff, later becoming mainly blackish brown, or pale grey-brown, or dirty creamy-white mottled brown, according to age. In soaring it has a regular vulture outline (see under Griffon Vulture) and widely spread primaries, but its size, *longer and wedge-shaped tail* (a distinctive feature at all ages) and relatively narrower wings coming more to a point prevent even the brown young bird being confused with the larger species. The shape of tail and wings also serve to distinguish young birds from the Hooded Vulture (*Necrosyrtes monachus*) which is of similar size and brown colour, common in parts of Africa. The beak is rather slender and weak. The bare skin of face and throat is yellow in adult, framed in a kind of hood of long pointed feathers; the head of young is greyish-brown. Bill darkish horn, tip black; legs greyish-white to pale yellow. Length about 24 ins. (61 cms.).

Habitat. Chiefly mountainous and hilly districts, but ranges widely over lowlands and in more primitive countries is often numerous about towns and villages. Haunts refuse dumps on outskirts of towns.

General Habits. Flight is much as Griffon Vulture, heavy and flapping when rising from the ground, but once under way planes along with rarely any active wing movement except at times a single very deep downward flap. It is more of a garbage eater than the larger vultures, but will also join Griffons at a carcass. Walks with long strides and body tilting from side to side. It is not usually sociable like Griffon, being generally met with singly or in pairs.

It is a very silent bird.

Food includes carrion, garbage, dead animals of any kind, decaying fruit, reptiles and small crustacea.

Status and Distribution. England—Two.

An immature bird shot near Kilve, Bridgwater Bay, Somerset, Oct. 1825.

Immature obtained Peldon, Essex, Sept. 28, 1868.

The race concerned, *Neophron percnopterus percnopterus*, breeds in S. Europe, N., E. and S. Africa, and Asia east to N.W. India; partial migrant. Another race occurs in India and Ceylon.

1959–1978 No additional records

GRIFFON VULTURE—*Gyps fulvus*

PLATE 10

When settled the Griffon Vulture is imposing from sheer size, but is ungainly, and ugly with its featherless head. On the wing, however, it is a most majestic bird, as it planes over a hillside with easy sweeping flight, with now and again a single powerful wing-beat, or soars on rigid wings in wide circles, often at a great height, the widely-spread primaries curving upwards at the tips. *The very broad, long wings with front and hind borders approximately parallel* for nearly the whole length and abruptly rounded off at the ends, with head and short broad tail projecting only a little beyond them, give a roughly rectangular outline when soaring, which with *general sandy colour* (often looking extremely pale in strong sunlight) contrasted with *black wing-quills and tail* is quite characteristic. On the other hand, in certain conditions against the light the whole bird can look as dark as a Black Vulture (*Aegypius monachus*). In direct flight the wings often appear distinctly angled. At close quarters a ruff round the neck can be distinguished, creamy-white in adults, brownish in immatures. Bill horn-coloured, tip and cere darker; legs grey. Length about 40 ins. (102 cms.).

Habitat. It frequents open country principally in mountainous districts, breeding in high crags, but ranges widely over lowlands.

General Habits. They are rather sociable, several often soaring together, and numbers roost and rest communally on high crags. They spend much of their time circling high overhead on the look-out for food, and one carcass will draw birds from a wide area owing to each observing the movements of others within its range of view. On the ground they form a jostling crowd round the carcass, moving with a clumsy waddling walk or in huge ungainly hops, aided by wings, when hurried.

It is in general very silent in the air or away from breeding-places.

Food is carrion of all kinds; in the case of large animals such as cattle there is often delay until putrefaction has set in.

Status and Distribution. British Isles—Three.

A young bird caught alive near Cork Harbour, Ireland, spring, 1843.

One seen near Southampton Water.

Two seen Ashbourne, Derby, June 4, 1927.

The race concerned, *Gyps fulvus fulvus*, breeds in S. Europe, W. Asia and N. Africa; it reaches central Africa in winter. Other races occur in India and S. Africa.

1959–1978 No additional records

PALLID HARRIER—*Circus macrourus*

PLATE 10

The adult male is a strikingly pale grey bird, some looking almost white at a little distance in strong sunlight. However, as Hen Harriers may also look very pale in similar circumstances and many individual Pallid Harriers are actually no paler on the upper-parts than Hens, the shade of grey is not always to be relied upon. Diagnostic characters are: *absence of pure white rump patch* (at very close quarters the rump is barred grey and white, but usually looks only a little paler than the back); *breast and sides of head nearly white*, instead of grey like upper-parts as in Hen Harrier; and, most important, there is *no black on the secondaries* whereas male Hen Harrier has a broad dark penultimate bar across the secondaries visible in flight (see sketch), and

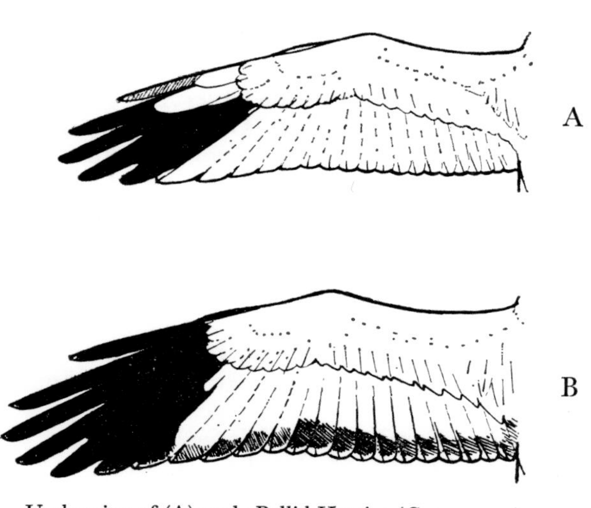

Underwing of (A) male Pallid Harrier (*C. macrourus*)
(B) male Hen Harrier (*C. cyaneus*)

Montagu's has a dark bar or bars across the middle of the secondaries visible at rest and in flight. In shape the wing is appreciably narrower than Hen Harrier's, more like Montagu's. The black of wing-tips is rather less extensive than in Hen Harrier and on the upper surface is less sharply demarcated from the grey, while on the under-side, if visible, it quickly tapers wedge-shaped into the white whereas in Hen the black and white meet in approximately a straight line. It is the only harrier which has the first primary appearing white in the field. Females and immatures closely resemble those of Hen Harrier, but the juvenile is distinguished from young Hen Harrier by having unstreaked rufous under-parts; they cannot

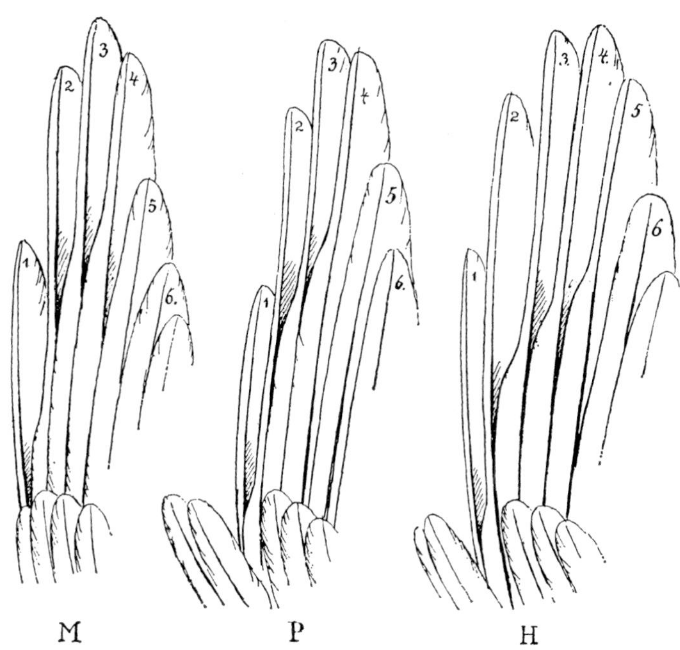

Primaries of M. Montagu's Harrier, *Circus pygargus*, P. Pallid Harrier, *C. macrourus*, H. Hen Harrier, *C. cyaneus*, to show differences in wing-formula and emarginations. In P and H primary-coverts are pushed aside to show emargination of 2nd visible primary, which they normally conceal, whereas in M this emargination is exposed. 5th visible primary in M and P is not emarginated and short, in H it is emarginated and longer.

be distinguished from those of Montagu's Harrier except by the position of the emargination of the second primary in relation to the wing-coverts (see diagram). As in Hen Harrier, bill is black with bluish base; cere and legs yellow. Length about 18 ins. (46 cms.).

Habitat. In the breeding season it occurs in much the same type of country as Hen Harrier, frequenting chiefly steppes and cornlands but also breeding regularly in marshes. In winter-quarters it frequents open grasslands and savanna.

General Habits are identical with those of Hen and Montagu's Harriers.

The female has a vibrating and distinctive cry "preee-pree-pri-pri".

Food includes mice and voles, small birds and chickens, eggs and nestlings, frogs and lizards.

Status and Distribution. Great Britain—Four.

Male shot Fair Isle, Shetland, May 8, 1931, after being present for at least a fortnight.

Adult male East Dorset, April 11, 1938.

Adult male seen Fair Isle for a week from May 6, 1942.

Immature male shot near Driffield, Yorks., Oct. 2, 1952.

The species breeds in S.W. Asia and E. Europe, occasionally westwards to Germany and Sweden. It winters chiefly in Africa, south to Cape, and in Asia to India, Ceylon and Burma. There are no subspecies.

1959–1978 No additional records. The Fair Isle record of 1942 is no longer accepted

SORA RAIL—*Porzana carolina*

PLATE 11

It is very like Spotted Crake (although a trifle smaller) and can be distinguished at a good view, when the *black face and stripe down the centre of breast, the sides of neck and upper breast without white spots* (but some on lower breast), and yellow or yellow-green bill without reddish base will identify it. Otherwise it is almost as Spotted Crake. The black of the face is less intense and the stripe down the throat less developed in female. The juvenile differs from juvenile Spotted Crake in having a whitish throat, not mottled or spotted. Legs are green. Length about 8 ins. (20 cms.).

Habitat. It frequents grassy marshes, wet meadows and swampy borders of rivers overgrown with rushes, etc., but not necessarily of large extent.

General Habits. Not so secretive as Spotted Crake, it is a considerably more familiar bird in the United States than the Spotted Crake is in the British Isles, occurring in large numbers in suitable places at times of migration, and being considered a regular game-bird. Otherwise its habits and behaviour appear to be almost exactly like those of Spotted Crake, and it swims and dives readily.

The characteristic whinny consists of about a dozen short, sweet, clear whistles. The first 8 or so are uttered very rapidly in an evenly descending scale, the remainder more deliberately and in a very uniform key; some harsher, more drawling notes often follow. In spring a plaintive whistled "ker-wee", and in autumn a sharp "keek" when disturbed.

Food consists of aquatic insects, small molluscs, crustacea, and in autumn largely seeds.

Status and Distribution. British Isles—Five.

One near Newbury, Berks., Oct. 1864.

One near Cardiff, Glamorgan, 1888.

Male, Tiree, Inner Hebrides, Oct. 25, 1901.

Immature male, Lewis, Outer Hebrides, Nov. 12, 1913.

Adult male Slyne Head lighthouse, Galway, April 11, 1920.

An American species breeding in southern half of Canada and much of U.S.A. except south and south-east, and wintering from California and South Carolina south to British Guiana, Venezuela and Peru. There are no subspecies.

1959–1978 One additional record

AMERICAN PURPLE GALLINULE—*Porphyrula martinica*

PLATE 11

A brilliantly coloured bird the size and shape of a Moorhen. Adult male and female have *head, neck and under-parts rich purple-blue*, with a bare pale blue shield on forehead, from bill to above eye; the rest of the *upper-parts are metallic olive-green*, bluer and paler on wings. *Under-tail coverts are always pure unbroken white* whereas those of Moorhen in all plumages are dark in the centre and white only at the sides, flashing as two white panels when the tail is flirted. The bill is bright red with a yellow tip; legs are yellow. Young birds in autumn (like that which reached Scillies in 1958) have back a glossy olive bronze, with wings rather greener, but are otherwise mainly brownish, becoming warm sandy buff on sides of head and on front of neck and breast, whitish on chin and belly; eye light brown, bill yellowish green at tip and reddish brown at base, forehead shield very dull green, legs dull orange-yellow. In this plumage it might perhaps be confused with an immature Moorhen. But in addition to the diagnostic difference in under-tail coverts mentioned above, the Moorhen is greyish, while the young Gallinule is a paler bird, sandier on breast and on sides of head, paler and much greener on mantle and especially on wings, with a deeper bill and larger shield; it lacks the characteristic flecked white line along the side of body which is early acquired by Moorhen. Length about 13 ins. (33 cms.).

[The Purple Gallinule of S. Europe (*Porphyrio porphyrio*) is an entirely different bird, considerably larger than a Coot with body plumage uniform dark purplish slate, and red legs and bill.]

Habitat. It frequents waters well supplied with low growing and floating vegetation such as water-lilies. Like Moorhen it can alight readily on branches and enter bushes, but normally keeps close to water and spends much time in the grass of the marshes.

General Habits. It swims and dives Moorhen-like, but frequently walks lightly and gracefully on floating water-plants, nodding and bowing its head and constantly flicking its tail displaying the white under-tail coverts; it usually moves with deliberation. Flight is normally low and feeble, with long yellow legs dangling, but long migration flights are regularly undertaken and vagrants not infrequently occur hundreds of miles outside the normal range.

Noisy much of the year, giving harsh shrill hen-like cacklings "hiddy-hiddy-hiddy, hit-up, hit-up, hit-up" starting rapidly and ending slowly; also a very guttural note.

Food includes insects, snails and other molluscs, frogs and worms, but probably consists chiefly of grain, especially rice, and seeds, and a little fruit is also taken.

Status and Distribution. England—One.

Immature found exhausted and later died, St. Mary's, Scilly Isles, Nov. 7, 1958.

The species breeds from U.S.A. (S. Carolina to Texas) and Mexico south to Peru and N. Argentine. It winters from south U.S.A. to N. Argentine. There are no subspecies.

1959–1978 No additional records

HOUBARA BUSTARD—*Chlamydotis undulata*

PLATE 9

It is about the size of a female Great Bustard. The most distinctive feature is the *white-fronted neck flanked with long tufts of black and white feathers*, which can be held close to the neck like ordinary plumage; the crest of elongated white crown-feathers with black tips is less conspicuous. In flight, unlike Little and Great Bustards, the *wing pattern is mainly darkish*, the chief feature being a black diagonal band running across the wing from the rear of the wing-root to the leading edge near the tip, with a band of white forward of this on the greater coverts and a ragged white patch surrounded by black near the base of the black primaries. The remainder of the wing is mottled sandy-brown like the rest of the upper-parts. There is a long greyish bib at the base of the neck. Summer and winter plumage do not differ; female and young closely resemble male. Flight is low and deliberate, the wing beating through a narrow angle above and below the horizontal (Little Bustard has a rapid whistling wing-beat mainly below the horizontal, and glides on bowed wings). Bill is brownish, legs straw-coloured. Length about 25 ins. (64 cms.).

Habitat. It frequents barren *Artemisia*-steppe or sandy plains and semi-desert, also cornfields and other cultivation.

General Habits. It has the stately attitude and gait of other bustards, but will at times walk with little mincing steps or with neck and body horizontal like Stone Curlew, and hunch itself to take advantage of cover; it also runs well and often does so in preference to flying. Outside the breeding season it chiefly occurs in small droves.

It is a very silent bird.

Food includes grass, leaves and, on breeding grounds, seeds and shoots of desert bushes. Animal matter includes insects, snails and lizards.

Status and Distribution. Great Britain—Four.

One Kirton-in-Lindsey, Lincs., Oct. 1847.

Adult male near Redcar, Yorks., Oct. 5, 1892.

Male near Spurn, Yorks., Oct. 17, 1896.

Female, St. Fergus, Aberdeen, Oct. 24, 1898.

The race concerned, *Chlamydotis undulata macqueenii*, breeds in extreme S.E. Europe and in W. Asia east to India and W. Siberia. Other races occur in the Sahara and Canary Is.

1959–1978 One additional record

BLACK-WINGED PRATINCOLE—*Glareola nordmanni*

PLATES 12 *and* 13

The Taxonomic Sub-committee of the British Ornithologists' Union in 1956 recommended "that *Glareola nordmanni* be treated as a colour phase of *Glareola pratincola*, being more or less dominant in south-east Europe and south-west Asia. *G. nordmanni* has been found breeding in Iraq alongside *G. pratincola*, from which it differs nowise in either habit or migration; the alleged shorter claws are not constant. In the Giza Zoological Museum are individuals intermediate between the two forms".

The reader is referred to *The Popular Handbook of British Birds* for details of the species' general appearance and habits.

The Black-winged form has the under-wing coverts black instead of chestnut, but the colouring is surprisingly hard to determine even when the bird is overhead; it is more visible on take off. The appearance of the upper-parts is a better guide: the typical Collared Pratincole shows considerable contrast between the blackish primaries and the paler inner wing and mantle, accentuated by the white trailing edge of the secondaries; the Black-winged bird has secondaries black like the primaries, and rather dark wing-coverts and mantle, giving an almost uniform effect.

Birds of the Black-winged form have occurred in England, Scotland and Ireland.

1959–1978 11 additional records. This bird is once again regarded as a full species, *Glareola nordmanni*, with five occurrences up to 1958

CASPIAN PLOVER—*Charadrius asiaticus*

PLATE 13

It is noticeably taller-standing than a Ringed Plover, with *much white and no black about the face; the pectoral band is light chestnut*, narrowly bordered black behind, in summer and drab in winter. In winter confusion is possible with Dotterel, but Caspian Plover is distinguished at once by (creamy-buff) *white-looking forehead*; this, continuous with the white of the broad eye-stripe and cheeks, gives a *white-faced appearance* even in flight, causing the dark band through the eye to stand out distinctively. Wing-bar is fainter than Ringed Plover's. Juvenile is much like adult in winter, but with buff edgings to the feathers of upper-parts and the white parts of the head more buff. The bird's upright, long-necked, stance is more like Golden Plover than Ringed Plover. Bill is black, legs are greenish or yellowish. Length about $7\frac{1}{4}$ ins. (18·5 cms.).

It should also be distinguished from the Greater Sand Plover (*Charadrius leschenaultii*) which has occurred in Sweden and Germany and which in winter plumage resembles the Caspian in colour and is not very much larger; but according to Elliott the Greater Sand Plover can be separated as much by Ringed Plover-like stance (see above) as by plumage, which is darker about the face and whiter below with a more sharply defined band across, or sometimes only on either side of, the breast.

Habitat. In winter-quarters is mainly an inland bird, frequenting open grasslands and bare or burnt patches, sometimes on water margins but often far from water. Nests on arid steppe or desert tracts, within reach of water, often saline.

General Habits. Behaviour appears to be much like Golden Plover's, but it can be very tame.

The flight note is a sharp "kwhit", sometimes a more spluttering "ptrrwhit".

Food is mainly insects.

Status and Distribution. England—Two.

Adult male shot and another bird seen near Great Yarmouth, Norfolk, May 22, 1890.

The race concerned, *Charadrius asiaticus asiaticus*, breeds in S.E. Europe and W. central Asia east to Semipalatinsk; another race occurs in E. central Asia. The western population winters in Persia, Arabia and E. Africa south to the Cape.

1959–1978 No additional records

SOCIABLE PLOVER—*Chettusia gregaria*

PLATE 13

It is not unlike a Lapwing, but without crest or metallic green back, the wings are not so round and broad, and the legs are longer. The upper-parts look drab in the field, *the crown is black, and a white stripe from forehead to nape is conspicuous; white secondaries are conspicuous in flight, and the tail is white with a black subterminal band.* In summer plumage the cheeks and lower throat are warm buff, the breast smoky, belly black shading to dark chestnut behind, and the under-tail coverts white. The primaries are black. In winter plumage the crown and eye-stripe are duller, less black and white, and the under-parts are white or whitish with some dark markings on the breast; immature birds are similar, but have a less uniform appearance above and the under-parts are more buff with dark streaks more pronounced on throat and breast. Bill and legs are black. Length about 11½ ins. (29 cms.).

Habitat. In winter-quarters it is recorded on open sandy or grassy plains and on waste ground near cultivation on dry uplands, but likes the vicinity of water. It nests in rather bare steppe country.

General Habits. Flight is not unlike Lapwing's, but it usually flies low. It is stated to spend much time on the wing and to be generally rather shy.

In winter-quarters a shrill short whistle and a harsh guttural note "kets" are recorded.

Food is chiefly insects.

Status and Distribution. British Isles—Five.

One near St. Michael's-on-Wyre, Lancs., autumn about 1860.

Female near Navan, Meath, Aug. 1, 1899.

One Tramore Bay, Waterford, Christmas 1909.

One North Ronaldsay, Orkney, Nov. 3, 1926.

One seen Northampton, Oct. 20, 1951.

The species breeds in S.E. Russia and central Asia, and winters from S. Russia to N.E. Africa, Arabia and India. There are no subspecies.

1959–1978 17 additional records

SEMIPALMATED SANDPIPER—*Calidris pusilla*

PLATE 14

The commonest small wader in eastern North America. In Europe it is only likely to be confused with a winter-plumaged Little Stint, being similar in size and having a white breast, dark legs and (at all seasons) grey upper-parts. It is best distinguished by its *heavier bill, thick at the base and markedly tapering*; it also has rather more coarsely-marked upper-parts, a less prominent wing-bar and a very different note. The *white of the throat extends back below the ear-coverts*, forming what one observer has described as a distinctive half-collar. In full breeding plumage the breast is prominently streaked with dark, but otherwise streaks are confined to the sides of the breast; immatures have breast more or less suffused with grey-buff, and are often slightly buffish or brownish above, though always unmistakably grey. For distinctions of Least, Western and Baird's Sandpipers see under those species. Bill black, legs very dark green, appearing black. Length about 6 ins. (15 cms.).

Habitat. Outside the breeding season it seems most at home on sea-beaches, but also frequents sand-flats of tidal estuaries, and to a lesser extent salt-marshes. During migration it is also found on shores of inland lakes. It is fonder of sandy shores than Least Sandpiper. Nests in arctic marshes and bogs.

General Habits. It has a peculiarly leisurely method of feeding, rather after the manner of a Knot. Feeds along the tide-line and on open flats by both picking and probing, also sometimes on rocks.

Flight note is a quick, husky "chrruk" or "chriip", less emphatic than Dunlin's; commonly modified to a soft "che". Another characteristic note is a short snappy "chip".

Food is chiefly insects, also molluscs, crustacea, worms, leeches and a few seeds.

Status and Distribution. Great Britain—Two.

One seen Cley, Norfolk, July 19, 1953.

One seen Isle of May, Fife, Sept. 19, 1957.

The species breeds on the arctic coasts of N. America south to S. coast of Hudson Bay, and winters from south U.S.A. to Chile and S. Brazil. There are no subspecies.

1959–1978 17 additional records

WESTERN SANDPIPER—*Calidris mauri*

PLATE 14

The most difficult of the American "peeps" to identify. It is smaller than a Dunlin and larger than a stint, but its long heavy bill suggests the former, and it is much less likely to be passed by as a Little Stint than is the Semipalmated Sandpiper. In winter plumage it is very similar to the Semipalmated, the upper-parts being grey with indistinct streaking; the breast white, sometimes faintly streaked with grey but always cleaner and whiter than a Dunlin's. There is a well-marked whitish eye-stripe and the head is often noticeably pale. The tail pattern resembles that of a Dunlin, but the wing-stripe is much less marked. Birds on passage in spring often show some *bright rufous on the ear-coverts and the sides of the crown and nape*, an important point of distinction from the Semipalmated. In full breeding plumage the whole upper-parts become bright rufous, suggesting a Little Stint, and the breast is well streaked. In autumn and winter most birds have bright *rufous edgings to the scapulars*, contrasting with the grey mantle; this is usually the best distinction from the Semipalmated, in which the scapulars are normally grey (a few individuals show dull cinnamon or orange buff). A few Westerns, however, have entirely grey backs and are very difficult to identify except by the bill; this is usually noticeably longer than the Semipalmated's (at least as long as head), fairly slender but thicker at base, slightly but noticeably *decurved at the tip* (see sketch), and is carried pointing more downwards. The bill-length varies considerably, however, and overlaps somewhat with that of the Semipalmated. The bird is slightly larger than the Semipalmated, and has a more upright stance and slightly longer legs. Both have partially webbed toes. Bill black, legs dark olive, but usually looking black. Length about 6½ ins. (16·5 cms.).

Habitat. It frequents the same type of habitats as Semipalmated Sandpiper. On passage it prefers exposed mudflats but also occurs to lesser extent on sandy beaches.

General Habits. In America it may occur in considerable numbers. Habits and actions are very like Semipalmated Sandpiper's, but it prefers to feed in deeper water. A confiding bird.

Call is a thin, shrill "chiet".

Food includes small crustacea and molluscs.

Top: Western Sandpiper (*Calidris mauri*).
Middle: Semipalmated Sandpiper (*Calidris pusilla*).
Lower: Least Sandpiper (*Calidris minutila*).

Status and Distribution. Scotland—One.
Seen and trapped Fair Isle, Shetland, May 28–June 3, 1956. (First recorded as Semipalmated Sandpiper.)

The species breeds in Alaska, and winters from south-east and south-west U.S.A. to Venezuela. There are no subspecies.

1959–1978 Five additional records

LEAST SANDPIPER—*Calidris minutilla*

PLATE 14

The smallest American wader, most likely to suggest a warmly-coloured Temminck's Stint, having a similar well-streaked breast and *pale yellowish or greenish legs*. It has, however, a *less marked wing-bar*, it lacks the white outer tail-feathers and its note is completely different. Summer adults and young are quite rufous-brown on the upper-parts, with dark streaks and light edgings producing a somewhat striped effect; when the leg colour cannot be distinguished they could be confused with Little Stint, but Least Sandpiper is always *darker and duller above*, lacks the prominent light V on the back of the young Little Stint and has prominent streaking on the breast. In abraded plumage in late summer can be very dark indeed. Length about 5½ ins. (14 cms.).

The pale legs, when visible, distinguish Least Sandpiper from all other small American waders. In addition: Western and Semipalmated Sandpipers, which are only slightly larger, have largely white breasts (except in full breeding plumage), grey, or grey-and-rufous, rather than brown upper-parts, and much thicker bills (see sketch on p. 57); White-rumped Sandpiper has similar streaked breast and is sometimes equally warm brown on upperparts, but is appreciably larger, with longer wings, and white rump in flight settles its identity.

Habitat. Outside the breeding season it haunts grassy and muddy places in marshes and round ponds, saltings and coastal mud-flats; unusual on sandy shores (unlike Semipalmated Sandpiper). Breeds on northern bogs or dry uplands.

General Habits. It is quiet and tame, and associates freely with other waders. General behaviour is much like Little Stint's, although liking for grassy ground suggests an approach to Temminck's.

Flight-note is a grating "kree-eet", distinguished by the "ee" sound from any note of Semipalmated Sandpiper, but an undistinctive "che" may also be given.

Food is insects, small crustacea, worms, molluscs, and sometimes considerable quantities of seeds.

Status and Distribution. Great Britain—Five.

One Mount's Bay, Cornwall, Oct. 10, 1853.

One near Bideford, Devon, Sept. 1869.

One near Mousehole, Cornwall, Sept. 1890.

One near Bideford, Devon, Aug. 22, 1892.

One shot Pool of Virkie, Shetland, Aug. 14, 1955.

An American species breeding from Alaska to Newfoundland and Nova Scotia, and wintering from western and southern U.S.A. south to Peru and Brazil. There are no subspecies

1959–1978 17 additional records, also a 1957 record now accepted

BAIRD'S SANDPIPER—*Calidris bairdii*

PLATE 14

A large American "stint" which could easily be passed by as a small, buffish Dunlin, but is best distinguished by its cleaner, *buff-and-white colouring, its long wings extending well beyond the tail* when at rest, and its almost complete *lack of wing-bar in flight.* Cheeks, sides of neck and breast-band are markedly buff, with indistinct brown streaks on sides of breast; there is little or no eyestripe. The upper-parts of immatures in autumn are rather pale buff-brown, with a prominent *scaly pattern* formed by whitish tips to the feathers, lacking the longitudinal streaks of similar species. Adults, however, lack the transverse scales and have a more variegated back pattern of brown, grey and buff. A slender, graceful bird with long neck and long wings emphasising its "horizontal" carriage. Bill black, markedly slender but longer than that of other stints; legs black. Length about 7 ins. (18 cms.).

In America Baird's Sandpiper is usually considered difficult to identify because of its lack of positive field marks. However, the long wings alone distinguish it from all similar species except the similarly-sized White-rumped Sandpiper, which is always much greyer and has a conspicuous white rump. The Pectoral Sandpiper is usually appreciably larger, has heavy breast-streakings forming a prominent gorget, a warmer brown, striped back and yellow legs. The smaller Semipalmated and Western Sandpipers can look scaly-backed and sometimes slightly buffish on breast, but are grey or rufous above, never strongly buff, and have much thicker bills. Buff-breasted Sandpiper can look somewhat similar, but has yellow legs and a very different shape and posture. Sanderling always has a prominent white wing-bar.

Habitat. Outside the breeding season it sometimes feeds on open flats, but prefers inland pools or places where muddy flats are partly overgrown with grass, or even uplands. Breeds chiefly on drier parts of tundra.

General Habits. These seem very much like others of the genus. It appears to feed mainly by picking on the surface rather than by probing.

The flight-note "krreep" is clearer and more trilled than that of other small American waders, recalling Curlew Sandpiper.

Food is crustacea, leeches, insects, also some vegetable matter.

Status and Distribution. Great Britain—Five.

One Hunstanton, Norfolk, Sept. 16, 1903.

Adult female St. Kilda, Outer Hebrides, Sept. 28, 1911.

One seen Perry Oaks, Middlesex, Sept. 17–22, 1950.

One seen Wicks, near Dungeness, Kent/Sussex, Sept. 19–27, 1952.

One seen Billinge Green, Cheshire, May 27–29, and three miles away on June 5, 1955.

The species breeds in N.E. Siberia and in northern N. America from Alaska to Baffin Land; it winters in S. America. There are no subspecies.

1959–1978 64 additional records

SHARP-TAILED SANDPIPER—*Calidris acuminata*

PLATE 15

It much resembles Pectoral Sandpiper, the chief difference being that the *markings on the breast do not form a distinct gorget*. In winter plumage the breast is only slightly streaked, chiefly at the sides. In summer the whole throat is closely spotted, with a coarser spotted and barred effect on breast and flanks, largely of bold V-shaped markings. Bill is blackish, legs are yellow-ochre or greenish. Length about 7½ ins. (19 cms.).

Habitat. In winter quarters it chiefly frequents shores of estuaries and lakes and fresh-water swamps; it is especially fond of grassy sides of lagoons and open wet marshy places.

General Habits. These seem to differ very little from Pectoral Sandpiper. It tends to rise with a twisting flight.

Note when flushed is a short soft metallic "pleep, pleep", or swallow-like "teet, teet, trrt, trrt".

Food includes insects, crustacea, molluscs, and some vegetable matter.

Status and Distribution. Great Britain—Five.

One Yarmouth, Norfolk, Sept. 1848.
One Caister, Norfolk, Sept. 16, 1865.
One Terrington marsh, Norfolk, Jan. 9, 1868.
One Breydon, Norfolk, Aug. 29, 1892.
One seen Hamilton, Lanarks., Oct. 18–21, 1956.

The species breeds in N.E. Siberia and occurs east to Alaska; it winters in S.E. Asia and Australia.

1959–1978 Ten additional records

STILT SANDPIPER—*Micropalama himantopus*

PLATE 15

A tall-standing bird, in size between Curlew Sandpiper and Reeve, with long dark greenish legs and long bill; the latter is 1½ times as long as the head, straight for most of its length but curving downward towards the tip. It is a distinctively dark grey bird in summer plumage, the *under-parts from breast to under-tail coverts prominently marked with dark grey transverse bars*; the fore-neck is streaked. It has a *rusty red stripe on the side of the head* from bill, through eye, to ear-coverts, and above this a pale super-ciliary stripe. The back and scapulars are greyish, boldly patterned after the manner of a Ruff, and the rump is banded like the under-parts. Migrants in July and August often retain most of the breeding plumage, but usually lack the red head-stripe. In winter plumage the whole bird is very much paler, with lightly streaked foreneck, and under-parts white. The *rump also becomes dull white* and the flight pattern, with uniform dark wings, is then not unlike Wood Sandpiper's; the feet project well beyond the end of the tail in flight. The pale stripe above the eye remains prominent. Other grey and white waders with which confusion is possible in autumn and winter are the dowitchers (which however have larger straight bills, shorter legs, and white not confined to rump but running up the back between wings like Spotted Redshank) and Lesser Yellowlegs (which is slightly larger, has speckled back and bright yellow legs). Length about 8 ins. (20 cms.).

Habitat. On passage it frequents coastal and other marshes, where it prefers fairly deep fresh-water pools; sometimes on open shores.

General Habits. When wading the bird prefers to be belly deep. Its feeding action is a perpendicular, sewing-machine motion like a Dowitcher, and the head is often submerged, but it is a relatively slow-moving, sedate bird.

A rather silent bird, sometimes giving a quiet "chu" or "tch-oowk-tchoowk" like a Knot or a weak Lesser Yellowlegs.

Food is mainly animal matter especially worms, but also includes seeds.

Status and Distribution. England—One.

One seen Spurn, Yorks., Aug. 31–Sept. 4, 1954.

The species breeds in Alaska and N. Canada west of Hudson Bay, wintering in S. America. There are no subspecies.

1959–1978 11 additional records

ESKIMO CURLEW—*Numenius borealis*

PLATE 15

It is not unlike Whimbrel, but is *smaller, with a shorter bill and without white rump*. The latter character would not, however, separate it from the American race of the Whimbrel, known as Hudsonian Whimbrel (*Numenius phaeopus hudsonicus*), an example of which occurred on Fair Isle on May 27–31, 1955. In flight the under surface of the wing of the Eskimo Curlew is conspicuously cinnamon buff, and the *primaries are uniformly dark without barring*. The dark crown has a light central stripe only obscurely indicated instead of prominent and sharply defined as in all forms of Whimbrel. Belly is buff. Legs are described as blue-grey or dark greenish. Total length about 13 ins. (33 cms.); bill about 2½ ins. (6 cms.).

Habitat. Breeding on the barren grounds of arctic America, with winter quarters chiefly the South American pampas. On migration it is said to have been rarely seen by water, visiting pastures, arable land, dunes and salt-marsh.

General Habits. Tame and unsuspicious on migration in N. America, it has been slaughtered almost to extinction. Flocks were fond of associating with Golden Plover. Habits were apparently similar to Whimbrel's.

Call-note in flight is a soft fluttering "tr-tr-tr".

Food in summer includes quantities of crowberries, but in autumn predominantly animal matter, mainly insects and some worms and molluscs.

Status and Distribution. British Isles—Seven.

Two near Woodbridge, Suffolk, Nov. 1852.

One Kincardine, Sept. 6, 1855.

One Dublin poultry market, Oct. 1870, said to have been shot Sligo.

One Aberdeen, Sept. 28, 1878.

One Kincardine, Sept. 21, 1880.

One Scilly Isles, Sept. 10, 1887.

An American species probably not quite extinct. It formerly bred in numbers in arctic Canada and wintered in S. America. There are no subspecies.

1959–1978 No additional records

MARSH SANDPIPER—*Tringa stagnatilis*

Plate 16

The pattern in flight, and winter plumage, closely resemble Greenshank's, but it is by no means merely a small edition of that bird. The main plumage difference is the marked paleness of the head, being *conspicuously white on the forehead and much of the face*. Smaller than a Redshank, the bird is altogether *slighter and more elegant than Greenshank*; the slender legs are relatively longer, so that the bird appears to stand higher off the ground, and they project noticeably further beyond the tail in flight; the bill is long and often looks of almost needle-like fineness. Summer plumage is really quite different, the back being boldly chequered and spotted with black on a buffish-grey ground. Bill is blackish, legs greenish. Length about 9 ins. (23 cms.).

Habitat. Outside the breeding season it occurs principally on freshwater marshes and marshy borders of pools and flooded cultivation; not much on the shore. It nests in grassy flats near marshes.

General Habits. Movements are quick, active and graceful. It often feeds like Greenshank with bill turned from side to side.

The note most frequently heard from migrants appears to be a rather feeble "tchick" or "tchu".

Food is chiefly aquatic insects and molluscs.

Status and Distribution. England—About twelve.

Chiefly in coastal localities in S.E. England from Sussex to the Wash, but there are records from Northumberland and Cheshire. Five have occurred in April or May, the remainder in autumn from August to October.

The species breeds in E. Europe and the western half of central Asia; it winters in Africa south to Cape and in S. Asia from Arabia to China. There are no subspecies.

1959–1978 13 additional records

GREATER YELLOWLEGS—*Tringa melanoleuca*

PLATE 16

A counterpart of Lesser Yellowlegs, one-third larger. *The relatively longer and stouter bill* is the only reliable field-mark, although the notes are usually distinguishable by persons acquainted with both species. The bill is stouter and considerably longer than Redshank's, and usually slightly, but distinctly, up-curved; it is in fact rather like Greenshank's, while Lesser Yellowlegs' is slenderer and shorter than Redshank's, or the same length, and straight or practically so. The general form and appearance are very much like Greenshank, although the pattern of the back is much more spotted, and it lacks a white wedge extending from upper tail-coverts up between wings. Size of body is of little value in the field to distinguish it from Lesser, but if both are together the Greater always stands higher owing to its longer legs. Bill is black with olive-green base, legs orange. Length about 12 ins. (30–31 cms.).

Habitat. Outside the breeding season, like Lesser Yellowlegs, it frequents grassy marshes, margins of ponds or lagoons, and coastal mud-flats.

General Habits. In flight its long neck and bill extended forward and its long yellow legs stretched out behind give it a slender, rakish appearance. It is wilder, more restless and noisy than Lesser Yellowlegs. Feeds entirely by snatching, never by probing, and is frequently seen running through water skimming the surface with its bill.

The three- or four-syllabled call "wheu-wheu-wheu" is very like Greenshank's, and is louder, clearer, higher-pitched, more ringing and modulated than the Lesser Yellowlegs' flatter and gentle "cu-cu".

Food is almost entirely animal matter: insects, snails, worms, crustacea and fish.

Status and Distribution. British Isles—About twelve.

Several have occurred in Ireland and Scilly Isles, also east to Kent and north to Shetland. There are some winter records (December and January), two in May, and the majority in autumn from late July to October.

The species breeds in N. America from Alaska to Newfoundland, and winters from western and southern U.S.A. to S. Argentine. There are no subspecies.

1959–1978 11 additional records

SOLITARY SANDPIPER—*Tringa solitaria*

PLATE 16

It is very like a rather small Green Sandpiper and has a similar *dark under-wing, but lacks white rump, and the tail when spread appears white at the sides with a dark centre.* Bill is blackish, legs are olive-green, rarely yellow. Length about $7\frac{3}{4}$ ins. (19·5 cms.).

Habitat. Outside the breeding season it frequents fresh waters in open or wooded country, with a liking for small stagnant pools, also muddy patches of wet meadows, gutters of salt-marsh, etc. Nests chiefly in wooded swamps.

General Habits. Flight is swift and darting; when alighting it drops down abruptly like a Snipe. Often flies in a zig-zag or jerky manner, and goes only a short distance when flushed. It is usually tame and unsuspicious, but in other ways behaviour is much like Green Sandpiper's.

Ordinary flight note is a distinctive, sharp "peet-weet" or "peet-weet-weet", thinner and less melodious than Green Sandpiper's. Less frequently heard is a quite distinct, fine "pit-pit-pit".

Food is largely insects, also snails, worms, and small crustacea, frogs and fish.

Status and Distribution. Great Britain—Six.

One banks of Clyde, Lanarks., some years previous to 1870.
One Scilly Isles, Sept. 21, 1882.
One near Marazion, Cornwall, Oct. 1884.
One seen Littlestone, Kent, July 18, 1908.
One seen Hickling, Norfolk, Aug. 1–2, 1942.
One seen Cley, Norfolk, Sept. 3–29, 1947.

The race concerned, *Tringa solitaria solitaria*, breeds from Labrador west across Canada to Yukon and south almost to Canadian–U.S.A. border. Another race breeds in N.W. North America. The species winters from south U.S.A. to Argentine.

1959–1978 12 additional records

TEREK SANDPIPER—*Xenus cinereus*

PLATE 17

On the ground it looks uniform rather pale brownish-grey above the whitish below. Long, dark, *noticeably upturned bill and bright orange-yellow legs* are distinctive. The folded wing may show a dark patch at the carpal joint, and can at times appear to be outlined with black. The upper-parts, including rump and tail, are uniform light grey in winter; the underparts white, with dusky streaks on breast, neck and sides of head. In summer irregular blackish markings on the sides of the mantle give a more or less distinct effect of two converging dark stripes on the back; the breast is more strongly streaked. There is some whitish round eye. As it rises the white tips to secondaries, white rump and pale outer tail-feathers produce a pattern a little like that of a very pale Redshank. Intermediate in size between Redshank and Curlew Sandpiper, its proportions are more those of an oversized Common Sandpiper. Bill (certainly in some breeding birds) is dark throughout. Length about 9 ins. (23 cms.).

Habitat. In winter-quarters it occurs chiefly on coastal flats and shores of tidal rivers; it is partial to pools on saltings. On migration it is sometimes found on fields far from water. Nests in northern marshes in grass or willow-scrub, also on islets.

General Habits. A lively bird, running about actively, much recalling a large Common Sandpiper in its carriage and behaviour; it often bobs the hind part of body up and down in a similar but more deliberate way, and has a comparable shallow flicking action in flight. It is not much inclined to associate with other species, and is often fairly tame and approachable.

Common call when flushed is a soft "twit-a-whit-whit-whit", and a sweet, quick "wee-wee-wee" has been noted from a migrant. On the breeding ground a liquid "koo-titroo" and various trillings.

Food includes aquatic insects and crustacea.

Status and Distribution. England—Three (but the 1951 records could refer to the same bird).

One seen Midrips, Sussex, May 30, 1951.

One seen Southwold, Suffolk, June 2–6, 1951.

One seen Teesmouth, Durham, Sept. 27–28, 1952.

The species breeds in Finland on Bothnian coast, N. and central Russia, and in Siberia, south to Semipalatinsk in Asia; it winters south to S. Africa, Malaya and Australia. There are no subspecies.

1959–1978 14 additional records

SPOTTED SANDPIPER – *Actitis macularia*

Plate 16

In many respects it closely resembles Common Sandpiper, and is the North American counterpart of that species, with which it has sometimes been treated as conspecific. Adults in summer are distinguished by *round black spots on under-parts,* and *mainly yellow bill* with dark tip. Immatures, and adults in winter, are hard to separate from Common Sandpiper and require close observation: D. I. M. Wallace has noted cleaner, colder, greyer tone of upper-parts, but *wing-coverts contrastingly barred* blackish and greyish-white; cleaner white front of neck; more evident narrow white trailing edge to secondaries in flight; tail usually without unbroken white outer margin, being dark blotched to edge. S. G. Madge has found the shorter tail diagnostic even in silhouette, also that the white wing bar is shorter than in Common Sandpiper and does not extend to inner secondaries. In autumn and winter the bill is tipped blackish with flesh or yellow base to lower mandible (all-dark in Common), and legs are relatively bright yellowish (not drab greenish). Length about 7½ ins. (19 cms.)

Habitat. Similar to Common Sandpiper, occurring at all seasons along margins of streams, swamps and other freshwaters, but also appears to frequent sea coasts, even sandy beaches, more regularly than Common. In some areas breeding sites are less regularly restricted to close vicinity of water and may be in grassland or cultivation, while birds sometimes feed in fields and gardens, although mainly at water's edge.

General Habits. Has Common Sandpiper's regular habit of teetering, or moving its rear end up and down when standing, or walking along shore line or log; also flies out low over water with similar shallow wing-beats and brief glide on down-bowed wings. Seldom more than one or two together. Tame and confiding.

Normal note is "peet-weet", softer than Common Sandpiper and without its ringing quality.

Food is mainly insects, including grasshoppers; worms, snails and fish fry also recorded.

Status and Distribution. British Isles—Six.

A pair Eastbourne, Sussex, Oct. 1866.

One near Finea, Co. Westmeath, Feb. 2, 1899.

One Hebden Bridge, Yorks., about 1899.

One seen Looe Bar, Cornwall, June 14, 1924.

One seen Cley, Norfolk, June 7–8, 1957.

The species breeds in N. America south to southern U.S.A., and winters south to Peru and S. Brazil. There are no subspecies.

1959–1978 41 additional records. A pair nested unsuccessfully in Scotland in 1975

WILSON'S PHALAROPE—*Phalaropus tricolor*

PLATE 17

Several distinctive features make this large phalarope unmistakable. At all seasons it has a *white rump, and lacks a white wing-bar*. In summer plumage the larger and brighter-coloured female has a pattern of broad stripes running down the neck and onto the back: starting as a black line through the eye, the bands on each side of the neck are dark chestnut, becoming paler on the back; the band over the crown to the centre of the back is pale, mainly bluish-grey. Under-parts are white with a red suffusion on the front of the neck; eye-stripe and lower cheeks are white. The duller male lacks the broad chestnut stripes, which are merely indicated by a cinnamon wash, and has a darkish crown and back. In winter both sexes are alike, with rather pale uniform brownish-grey upper-parts and white under-parts, the strikingly white unstreaked breast and flanks being conspicuous at a considerable distance when the bird is ashore. The sides of the head and neck are also mainly white, sometimes with a short dark mark through the eye. In flight both rump and tail appear white. Body can sometimes look portly compared with the thin neck and delicate head and bill. It most closely resembles Lesser Yellowlegs, with which it often associates, but lacks the back-spotting of that species and can usually be picked out by its actions. Bill is strikingly slender, straight and blackish, as long as a Reeve's but not so long as a Redshank's. Legs are black in summer, but in winter are often yellowish. Length about 9 ins. (23 cms.).

Habitat. In winter quarters it is largely a marsh, shore and lake bird. Although it may be seen on the open water of lakes, unlike other phalaropes shuns the open sea. Nests in grass in or near marshy ground.

General Habits. It is much less aquatic than the other phalaropes and although it swims freely, more time is spent ashore like a typical wader, feeding on muddy margins or wading in the shallows. It is a very active bird on land, always running about when feeding with a curious lurching gait, and darting its bill from side to side or forwards almost continuously. On the water it rears up to feed in typical phalarope manner, otherwise swims rather deep with horizontal back. It will spin not only on water but on land also.

It has a nasal, grunting note, "aangh" and a Yellowlegs-like "chu" in flight.

Food is mainly insects and some seeds.

Status and Distribution. Great Britain—Three (but the 1958 records could refer to the same bird).

One seen Rosyth, Fife, Sept. 11–Oct. 5, 1954.

One adult female seen near Shefford, Beds., May 10–13, 1958.

One adult female seen Malltraeth Lake, Anglesey, June 15–16, 1958.

The species breeds from central Canada south to central California, Iowa and Indiana; it winters in southern S. America. There are no subspecies.

1959–1978 94 additional records

GREAT BLACK-HEADED GULL—*Larus ichthyaetus*

PLATE 18

Its *great size* (as large as Great Black-back), *black hood in breeding plumage, heavy orange bill with blackish subterminal band, and greenish legs* are distinctive. The crimson ring round the eye is conspicuous. The ends of the primaries are black with white tips. In winter plumage the head is white with blackish streaks on the crown and dark marks in front of and behind the eye. Juvenile has mantle dark brown with whitish feather-edgings, head paler, both primaries and secondaries blackish with pale tips, and white tail with broad almost terminal blackish band; bill blackish and legs greyish. In first-year birds the wings and tail are as juvenile, back grey more or less marked with brown; in second year primaries are still much like juvenile, with white tips little developed, tail still with black band, and black hood developed in summer but flecked with white; third year almost as adult, but more black in primaries and tail. Length about 25 ins. (64 cms.).

Habitat. Outside the breeding season it occurs on sea coast, and on large rivers and lakes inland. Nests on river deltas and steppe lakes.

General Habits. Behaviour is much like other large gulls. It is described as a ruthless pirate, attacking smaller gulls when in possession of food.

Usual note is a harsh, almost corvine "kra-ah".

Food is mainly fish, but it also takes reptiles, crustacea and insects.

Status and Distribution. England—Five.

Adult off Exmouth, Devon, end May or early June 1859.

One seen Telscombe Cliffs, Sussex, Jan. 4, 1910.

One seen Bournemouth, Hants., Nov.–Dec., 1924.

One seen Cromer, Norfolk, March 2–9, 1932.

One seen Hove, Sussex, Aug. 9, 1932.

The species breeds in S. Russia and central Asia, and winters south to E. Mediterranean, Red Sea, India and Burma. There are no subspecies.

1959–1978 Two additional records

BONAPARTE'S GULL—*Larus philadelphia*

PLATE 18

Resembles Black-headed Gull in having white fore-wing and black ends of primaries, but differs in smaller size (but not so small as Little Gull), *thinner black bill and, in summer plumage, a dark slate-coloured hood.* In winter the head is like Black-headed Gull's at the same season. The best mark at all ages is the *white underside to the primaries* (dark greyish in adult Black-headed, dusky in first winter). Legs are orange in adult (not red, like Black-headed) but dusky in juvenile. Juvenile is much like small juvenile Black-headed Gull, but with black patches near the ends of the inner primaries and secondaries. First-year birds are like winter adults, but with wings and tail as juvenile and generally more or less grey on the head in summer. Length about 12½ ins. (32 cms.).

Habitat. Outside the breeding season, like Black-headed Gull it frequents bays, harbours, estuaries and coastal lagoons, or rivers, lakes and swamps inland; it also feeds on arable land and fields. Nests near water in spruce forest belt.

General Habits. Flight is tern-like, with the body lifted perceptibly at each stroke of the wings. It feeds largely by picking food from surface of water, also while swimming, and sometimes dives from the air; it also frequently takes insects in the air.

As a rule silent, but occasionally emits a harsh rasping cry.

Food is crustacea, worms, small fish and insects.

Status and Distribution. British Isles—About eleven.

Only once recorded from Ireland. Over half the records come from the south coast of England from Cornwall to Sussex, but there are two from N. England and one Scotland. The bird has been found most frequently in winter between October and February; there are also records in April, June, July and August.

The species breeds in central and N. Canada and Alaska; it winters on Pacific and Atlantic coasts of U.S.A. and Mexico. There are no subspecies.

1959–1978 19 additional records

ROSS'S GULL—*Rhodostethia rosea*

PLATE 18

It could be recognized by the small and delicate bill, *wings without black (except on outer web of first primary), graduated tail, and in summer by the narrow black ring round the neck.* The head in summer, under-parts, rump and tail are white, tinged rosy; back is pearl-grey. The head in winter is tinged grey with some dark mottlings round the eye. The wings are long and pointed, extending far beyond the tail when at rest. Bill is black, feet red. Juvenile has the back mottled brownish-black and pale buffish-grey, the dark feathers having light margins, crown and nape blackish, forehead and sides of head whitish with dusky markings round and behind the eye, tail white with black terminal band, under-parts white with dusky pectoral band; the outer primaries are black, the inner ones white with black ends decreasing in size up to wholly white secondaries, the wing-coverts much as back. This wing-pattern is much like young Sabine's Gull, whose forked tail, lighter back and wholly white inner primaries should, however, at once distinguish it. First winter birds have crown and back grey, but wings and tail as juvenile. Length about 12½ ins. (32 cms.).

Habitat. Migratory birds in autumn frequent sea-coast and neighbouring lagoons, much like other gulls. In the breeding-season it frequents pools and islands of swampy tundra in deltas of arctic rivers.

General Habits. Flight has been compared to a tern's or

Kittiwake's. Not shy. The birds rest regularly on the sea-ice or the edge of glaciers; apparently rarely observed swimming.

Notes are variable, high-pitched and more melodious than those of most gulls; they include "a-wo, a-wo, a-wo", and "claw, claw, claw" (or "cliaw, cliaw").

Food includes insects, small fish and crustacea.

Status and Distribution. Great Britain—Two.

One near Tadcaster, Yorks., Dec. 22, 1846 or Feb. 1847.

Immature caught between Whalsay and Skerries, Shetland, April 28, 1936.

An arctic species breeding in N.E. Siberia and probably also Greenland; recorded in summer from Spitzbergen, Novaya Zemlya and other arctic islands. Migrates to Kamchatka and N. Alaska. There are no subspecies.

1959–1978 20 additional records

ROYAL TERN—*Sterna maxima*

Plate 19

About the size of a Common Gull, the Royal Tern is considerably larger than any of the terns breeding in this country and confusion is only likely with Caspian Tern; both have a pale grey back, white rump, tail and under-parts, black crown in full breeding plumage, black legs and reddish bill. On the wing the best distinction at all seasons is the Royal Tern's *relative lack of blackish on the primaries, particularly on the under-wing*: here it is inconspicuous being confined to a darkening towards the primary tips, whereas in the Caspian Tern the whole of the under-surface of the primaries is dark, forming a distinct contrast with the white under-wing coverts. Other points of difference are: the bill of the Royal Tern is *rather paler, more orange*, and a little less heavy than that of Caspian; the Royal is a slightly smaller bird but its *tail is more deeply forked*; the Royal Tern's crown and forehead are black only in the early part of the breeding season, and before nesting is over the forehead is white, the white extending over much of the crown by autumn, whereas the Caspian Tern never has a white forehead or crown as these parts are streaked dark in autumn and winter; the Royal's crown is considerably the more crested. Legs blackish. Length about 18–20 ins. (46–51 cms.).

Habitat. It is mainly maritime, and unlike Caspian Tern is very rare inland. It breeds only in coastal localities, frequenting sandy islands, sand bars, inlets and lagoons, and in winter harbours and estuaries as well as more open shallow coasts.

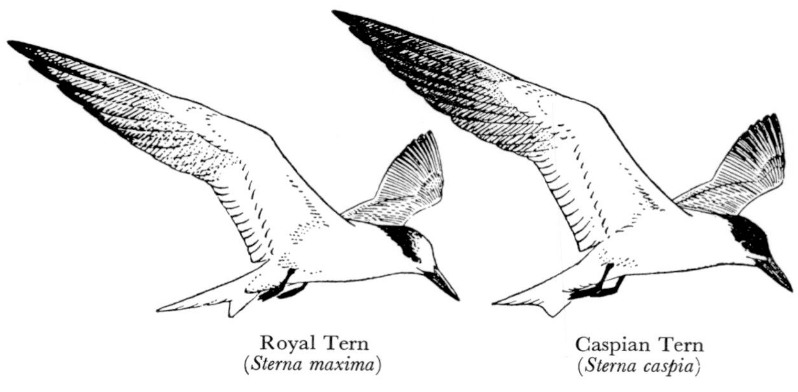

Royal Tern (*Sterna maxima*) Caspian Tern (*Sterna caspia*)

General Habits. Flight is swift and strong, but more leisurely when fishing. When diving from air for food it usually submerges completely, and it seldom swims on the surface. Is highly gregarious in summer, breeding in dense and often mixed colonies; at other seasons it may occur in small flocks or even singly.

Call is "keer", higher pitched and less raucous than that of Caspian Tern.

Food is chiefly small fish, also crabs, shrimps and other crustacea.

Status and Distribution. Ireland—One.

The remains of a bird long dead found North Bull, Dublin, March 24, 1954.

The bird breeds in West Indies, in U.S.A. from Maryland to Texas and on Pacific coast in Lower California and Mexico; it also frequents most of the coast of West Africa apparently throughout the year. In America it winters from California and N. Carolina south to Peru and Argentine.

1959–1978 Three additional records

BRIDLED TERN—*Sterna anaethetus*

PLATE 19

Although credited with being difficult to distinguish from the Sooty Tern, the Bridled's *dark greyish brown* (not sooty black) *back and wings, and, even more, its evidently smaller size,* makes discrimination in life quite feasible, especially if the two species are about together at close quarters and in good light; on dull days the upper parts of the Bridled look blackish. It also differs from Sooty Tern in having the white of the fore-head prolonged backwards in a *superciliary stripe which extends behind the eye.* Bill and legs are blackish. Young in first winter are much as adult, but with the crown more streaked white. Length about 13–14 ins. (33–36 cms.).

Habitat. Like Sooty Tern it is a pelagic species, coming inshore to rocky and sandy, scrubby islands only in the breeding season.

General Habits. It is swifter and more graceful in flight than Sooty Tern and differs from it in having water-repellent plumage so that it can sit on the water; in practice it settles more readily on driftwood and buoys. Otherwise habits appear to be much like those of Sooty Tern, and like that bird it does not dive into the water.

Its notes are quite distinct from Sooty Tern's. The usual call is a yapping "wep-wep" or "wup-wup"; when fishing, harsh grating and prolonged notes "karr", "k-ow", "k-arr"; at times a subdued "kwit".

Food is mainly fish, crustacea and molluscs.

Status and Distribution. British Isles—Four.

One found dead Dungeness, Kent, Nov. 19, 1931.

One found dead North Bull, Dublin, Nov. 29, 1953.

One found dead Gower, Glamorgan, Sept. 11, 1954.

One found dead near Weston-super-Mare, Somerset, Oct. 17, 1958.

The race concerned, *Sterna anaethetus fuligula,* breeds in the Indian Ocean and neighbouring seas from Australia to Red Sea, and perhaps W. Africa. Other races occur in the Caribbean and Pacific.

1959–1978 One additional record

SOOTY TERN—*Sterna fuscata*

PLATE 19

A tern with *sooty-black upper-parts and band from base of the bill to the eye, white under-parts and a white forehead.* For distinctions from Bridled Tern, see that species. In both species the tail is deeply forked, the outer web of the long outer feathers is white. Bill and legs blackish. Summer and winter plumages do not differ. Young birds in first winter have the whole upper-parts sooty-brown, back flecked with white, and grey-brown under-parts, and the juvenile is much the same. Length about 14–15 ins. (36–38 cms.).

Habitat. In contrast to the other terns, the Sooty Tern and its allies are essentially pelagic, only coming to land to breed on islands and reefs and even then generally fishing out of sight of land.

General Habits. Flight is firmer and more steady than Common Tern's, more like the larger terns. It sometimes soars high in air. Feeds on fish and other organisms at the surface, sweeping down to pick them up as it flies instead of plunging like most of the terns. When not engaged in nesting duties it seems to be nearly constantly on the wing, rarely settling on stakes, buoys, etc., and hardly ever on the water.

Common flight-notes are a squeaky quack and a clearly enunciated high-pitched "ker-wacki-wack".

Food is chiefly small fish.

Status and Distribution. Great Britain—About sixteen.

There are records from S., E., and W. coasts north to Orkney, also several inland. The dates extend from March or April to October.

The race concerned, *Sterna fuscata fuscata*, breeds in tropical waters in Caribbean, Atlantic, Indian Ocean, and China Sea to Australia; other races occur in the Pacific.

1959–1978 Seven additional records

RUFOUS TURTLE DOVE—*Streptopelia orientalis*

PLATE 20

It closely resembles Turtle Dove, but is *larger and considerably darker, both above and below*. The tail is probably the best character: dark and graduated like Turtle Dove's, it is edged with pale grey (not white) and broadly tipped with blue-grey (not white) on all except the central tail feathers; these latter are narrowly tipped blue-grey whereas in Turtle Dove they are dark to the end. The under tail-coverts are also grey instead of white. The blue-grey, instead of white, tips to the feathers of the neck-patch would only be visible at close range. Length about 13 ins. (33 cms.).

Habitat. A forest dove, breeding in deep forest, but otherwise mostly seen in more open and cultivated areas in wooded country.

General Habits. These are substantially similar to Turtle Dove's. It will flight a considerable distance to feed, but does not normally form flocks.

The call is a dull sleepy drone of four notes "croo croo-croo croooo".

Food includes rice.

Status and Distribution. England—Two.

Immature near Scarborough, Yorks., Oct. 23, 1889.

Immature female shot Castle Rising, Norfolk, Jan. 29, 1946.

The race concerned, *Streptopelia orientalis orientalis*, breeds from Tibet and Siberia east to Japan. Other races occur in Riu Kiu Islands, India and central Asia.

1959–1978 Six additional records

GREAT SPOTTED CUCKOO—*Clamator glandarius*

PLATE 20

A striking-looking bird with *crested head and long tail*. The crown and sides of head are rather dark grey, sharply demarcated from the yellowish-cream of the throat, which is prolonged backwards below ear-coverts as a sort of partial collar. The rest of the upper-parts are dark brown spotted with white. In flight broad white tips of the coverts, giving a *boldly spotted appearance to the wing*, are striking; the long white-edged tail, and to a lesser extent the rounded wings, have Magpie-like proportions. The general appearance is not hawk-like as Cuckoo. The sexes are similar; young have head and nape nearly black, with rufous on the wings. Total length about 15–16 ins. (38–41 cms.); tail about 7–8 ins. (18–20 cms.).

Habitat. It frequents open forest, wood-borders, olive-groves, and bushy country with or without scattered trees.

General Habits. In Spain in early summer it is a conspicuous bird, flying about freely in the open with moderately rapid, dipping flight, perching on bushes, fences and buildings, as well as in trees, and calling freely; usually in association with Magpies which are its favourite nest-host, and breeding often in groups. In early spring it is stated to be silent and difficult to see or to dislodge from trees. On the ground it hops in rather awkward fashion.

The spring call is a very rasping "keeow-keeow-keeow-keeow". It has also a short harsh "cark, cark" of warning or alarm.

Food is almost entirely insects.

Status and Distribution. British Isles—Eight.

One Omey Island, Galway, about March 1842.

One near Bellingham, Northumberland, Aug. 5, 1870.

One Yarmouth, Norfolk, Oct. 18, 1896.

One seen Skellig Rock, Kerry, April 30, 1897.

One found dead Cahersiveen, Kerry, early spring 1918.

One seen Hickling, Norfolk, July 29, 1941.

One found dead near Aberdovey, Merioneth, April 1, 1956.

Immature found dead Winterton, Norfolk, Aug. 6, 1958.

The species breeds in S.W. and S.E. Europe, in Asia east to Persia, and in N., E. and S. Africa; it winters in tropical and S. Africa. There are no subspecies.

1959–1978 14 additional records. The Kerry record of 1897 is no longer accepted

BLACK-BILLED CUCKOO—*Coccyzus erythrophthalmus*

PLATE 20

It resembles the Yellow-billed Cuckoo in general appearance but is distinguished from it by *absence of bright rufous on the wings, no black and much less white in the tail*, and at close quarters, by black bill and red ring round eye (yellowish in autumn immature). Viewed from below, the throat is a rather darker shade than that of Yellow-billed. Length about 11 ins. (28 cms.).

Habitat. In the breeding-season it frequents wood-borders, thickets, bushy roadsides, orchards, or cultivated grounds.

General Habits. Habits are similar to Yellow-billed Cuckoo's and it moves in the same characteristic loping fashion.

"Song" resembles Yellow-billed Cuckoo's, but is distinguished by being rather soft and gurgling, instead of harsh and rattling, with notes delivered in even time, not retarded, and formed of series of two to five note phrases, "ka-ka" etc.

Food is almost entirely insects.

Status and Distribution. British Isles—Four.

One Killead, Antrim, Sept. 25, 1871.

One Tresco, Scilly Isles, Oct. 27, 1932.

Immature found dead near Southend, S. Kintyre, Nov. 8, 1950.

Exhausted bird caught Foula, Shetland, Oct. 11, 1953.

This American species breeds east of the Rockies, in S. Canada and N. and central U.S.A.; it winters in N.W. South America. There are no subspecies.

1959–1978 Three additional records

HAWK OWL—*Surnia ulula*

PLATE 21

It is as much diurnal as nocturnal. *Short pointed wings and long tail give the bird a hawk-like appearance in flight.* It has a characteristic habit of *perching on an exposed, elevated position,* such as bare pole or top of a dead fir-tree. The crown is blackish, closely spotted white; rest of the upper parts mottled and barred blackish-brown and white, the under-parts white narrowly barred blackish; the facial disk is incomplete (not extending above eye), greyish, bordered black at back. Length about 14–15 ins. (36–38 cms.).

Habitat. It normally frequents northern conifer-forests, and extends into the birch zone on fells.

General Habits. It is usually fearless of man. Commonly sits not upright, as do most owls, but with body inclined forwards, and frequently jerks up its tail. Flight is swift and hawk-like, but has the soft, noiseless character common to other owls. It takes small birds on the wing.

Note is chattering and hawk-like; often uttered in flight, as well as when settled.

Food is chiefly small mammals and some insects.

Status and Distribution. Great Britain—Eight.

One off Cornwall, March 1830.
One Yatton, Somerset, August 1847.
One Unst, Shetland, winter 1860–1.
One Maryhill, Lanark, December 1863.
One near Greenock, Renfrew, November 1868.
One Amesbury, Wilts., prior to 1876.
One Gight, Aberdeen, Nov. 21, 1898.
One Northants., Oct. 19, 1903.

The above records include examples both of the European race (*Surnia ulula ulula*—1876, 1898) and of the American race (*Surnia ulula caparoch*—1830, 1847, 1863). The former breeds in Scandinavia, Finland, N. Russia and Siberia, in Europe wintering south to Germany and S. Russia; the latter breeds in Canada and Alaska, wintering south to the Canadian border. Another race occurs in central Asia.

1959–1978 Two additional records

PLATE
1

p. 17

Juv. *Ad. m. summer*
WHITE-BILLED DIVER (*ca.* $^{1}/_{9}$)

p. 19

Ad.
BLACK-BROWED ALBATROSS (*ca.* $^{1}/_{10}$)

p. 20

Ad.
CAPPED PETREL (*ca.* $^{1}/_{9}$)

PLATE
2

p. 21

Ad.
BULWER'S PETREL (*ca.* 1/4)

p. 22

Madeiran *Ad. f.* Cape Verde *Ad. m.*
LITTLE SHEARWATER (*ca.* 1/4)

p. 23

Ad. f. *Ad. f.*
WILSON'S PETREL (*ca.* 1/4) WHITE-FACED PETREL

Ad.
MADEIRAN PETREL (*ca.* 1/4)

p. 24

Ad. m. *Ad. f.*
MAGNIFICENT FRIGATEBIRD (*ca.* 1/20)

p. 25

PLATE 4

Juv. Ad. m. summer
CATTLE EGRET
(*ca.* 1/7)

p. 27

Ad. winter Ad. m. summer
GREAT WHITE
EGRET (*ca.* 1/14)

p. 28

Ad. *Ad.* *Juv.*
RED-BREASTED GOOSE (*ca.* 1/10)

p. 30

p. 31

Ad. m. *Ad. f.*
BAIKAL TEAL (*ca.* 1/6)

p. 32

Ad. m. *Ad. f.*
BLACK DUCK (*ca.* 1/7)

p. 33

Ad. m. *Ad. f.*
BLUE-WINGED TEAL (*ca.* 1/8)

p. 35

Ad. m. *Ad. f.*
RING-NECKED DUCK (*ca.* 1/7)

p. 36

Ad. f. *Ad. m.* *Juv.*
STELLER'S EIDER (*ca.* 1/8)

p. 37

Ad. m. *Ad. f.* *Ad. m. eclipse*
HARLEQUIN DUCK (*ca.* 1/8)

p. 39

Ad. m. *Ad. f.* 1*st. winter m. moulting (upper)*
BUFFLEHEAD (*ca.* 1/8)

p. 40

Ad. f. *Ad. m.*
HOODED MERGANSER (*ca.* 1/8)

p. 51

Ad. m. *Ad. m.*
HOUBARA BUSTARD (*ca.* 1/8)

p. 43

Ad. m. *Juv.*
EGYPTIAN VULTURE (*ca.* 1/10)

p. 42

Ad. m. *Ad. f.*
BLACK KITE (*ca.* 1/7)

PLATE 9

p. 44

Juv. *Ad. m.*
GRIFFON VULTURE (*ca.* 1/12)

p. 46

Ad. f. *Ad. m.*
PALLID HARRIER (*ca.* 1/6)

p. 48

Ad. m. summer *Ad. f. winter* *Juv. m.*
SORA RAIL (*ca.* 1/4)

p. 49

Imm. *Ad.*
AMERICAN PURPLE GALLINULE (*ca.* 1/8)

Drawn by P. J. Hayman

(*Upper*) COLLARED PRATINCOLE (*Glareola pratincola*)
(*Lower*) BLACK-WINGED PRATINCOLE (*Glareola nordmanni*)

These sketches are designed to show that there are more striking differences in the field between typical specimens of the two species than the colour of the under-wing, which is often difficult to determine. The Collared Pratincole has a strongly contrasting wing-pattern with pale inner primaries and secondaries, and a white trailing edge to the latter. The Black-winged has more uniformly dark upper-parts which contrast more with the rump, while the whole bird has a more black-and-white appearance.

M. winter *Ad. m. summer* Collared Pratincole *ad. m. summer*
BLACK-WINGED PRATINCOLE (*ca.* 1/4)

p. 52

Ad. f. winter *Ad. m. summer* *Juv. m.*
CASPIAN PLOVER (*ca.* 1/4)

p. 53

Juv. m. *Ad. m. summer*
SOCIABLE PLOVER (*ca.* 1/5)

p. 54

p. 58 & p. 55

Juv. m. *Ad. m. winter* *Juv. m.* *Ad. m. winter*
LEAST SANDPIPER (*ca.* 1/4) SEMIPALMATED SANDPIPER

p. 56

Spring *Autumn*
WESTERN SANDPIPER (*ca.* 1/3)

p. 59

Ad. f. summer *Ad. f. winter* *Juv. m.*
BAIRD'S SANDPIPER (*ca.* 1/4)

p. 60

Ad. winter *Ad. summer* *Juv.*
SHARP-TAILED SANDPIPER (*ca.* 1/4)

p. 61

Ad. summer *Ad. winter*
STILT SANDPIPER (*ca.* 1/3)

p. 62

Ad. m. summer *Ad. m. summer*
ESKIMO CURLEW (*ca.* 1/8) SLENDER-BILLED CURLEW

PLATE 16

p. 63

Ad. m. winter *Ad. m. summer*
MARSH SANDPIPER (*ca.* 1/5)

p. 64

Juv. m. *Ad. m. summer*
GREATER YELLOWLEGS (*ca.* 1/5)

p. 67
&
p. 65

Ad. f. summer *Juv. m.* *Ad. m. summer*
SPOTTED SANDPIPER (*ca.* 1/5) SOLITARY SANDPIPER

p. 66

Juv. m. *Ad. f. summer*
TEREK SANDPIPER (*ca.* 1/4)

p. 69

Ad. f. summer *Winter* *Ad. m. summer*
WILSON'S PHALAROPE (*ca.* 1/4)

PLATE 18

p. 70

Juv. f. *Ad. m. summer* *Ad. f. winter*
GREAT BLACK-HEADED GULL (*ca.* 1/10)

p. 71

Juv. m. *Ad. m. winter* *Ad. f. summer*
BONAPARTE'S GULL (*ca.* 1/10)

p. 72

1*st winter f.* *Ad. summer* *Ad. winter*
ROSS'S GULL (*ca.* 1/10)

Ad. spring *Ad. autumn*
ROYAL TERN (*ca.* 1/6)

p. 73

Ad. m. summer *Juv. f. (upper)* *Juv.* *Ad. m. summer (upper)*
BRIDLED TERN (*ca.* 1/6) SOOTY TERN

p. 75
&
p. 76

PLATE 20

p. 77

Juv. f. *Ad. f.*
RUFOUS TURTLE DOVE (*ca.* 1/6)

p. 77

1*st summer f.* *Ad. m.*
GREAT SPOTTED CUCKOO (*ca.* 1/6)

p. 79

Ad. m. *Ad. f.*
BLACK-BILLED CUCKOO YELLOW-BILLED CUCKOO (*ca.* 1/5)

Ad. m. *Ad. f.*
HAWK OWL (*ca.* 1/6)

p. 80

Egyptian *(lower)* Red-necked *Ad. m. (middle)* Common Nighthawk *Ad. m. (upper)*
NIGHTJARS (*ca.* 1/3)

p. 81
&
p. 82

PLATE
22

p. 83

Ad. m. NEEDLE-TAILED SWIFT (*ca.* 1/5) *Ad. f.* ALPINE SWIFT

p. 84

Ad. BLUE-CHEEKED BEE-EATER (*ca.* 1/3) *Juv.*

p. 85

Ad. *Juv.*
LESSER SHORT-TOED LARK (*ca.* 1/3)

p. 86

Juv. m. *Ad. m.* *Ad. f.*
RED-RUMPED SWALLOW (1/3)

p. 87

F. winter *M. summer* *Juv.*
PECHORA PIPIT (1/3)

p. 88

Ad. m. *Imm.* *Ad. f*
CITRINE WAGTAIL (*ca.* 2/5)

Juv. *Ad. f. (upper)* *Ad. m.* Eastern race (*lower*)
RUFOUS BUSH ROBIN (*ca.* 1/3)

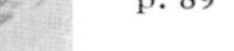

p. 89

Ad. f. *Ad. m. (upper)* *Juv.*
NIGHTINGALE (1/3) THRUSH NIGHTINGALE

p. 90

Juv. m. *Ad. m.* *Ad. f.*
RED-FLANKED BLUETAIL (*ca.* 1/2)

p. 92

PLATE
26

p. 94
&
p. 93

Ad. m. winter (upper). 1*st summer m. Ad. f. (lower right)* Isabelline. *Ad. m. (upper)*
PIED WHEATEAR (1/3) ISABELLINE WHEATEAR

p. 95

Eastern. *Ad. m.* *Ad. f.* *Ad. m.* Western. *Ad. m.* *(lower)*
DESERT WHEATEAR (1/3)

p. 96

N. African. *Ad. m. (upper). Ad. f.* Typical. *Ad. m. (upper). Ad. f.*
BLACK WHEATEAR (1/3)

p. 97

1st winter f. *Ad. m. summer* *Ad. m. winter (upper)*
ROCK THRUSH (1/3)

P. 98

Imm. m. moulting *Ad. m.* *Ad. f.*
SIBERIAN THRUSH (*ca.* 1/4)

p. 100 & p. 101

Ad. *Imm.*
SWAINSON'S THRUSH (*ca.* 1/4) GREY-CHEEKED THRUSH

PLATE 28

p. 102

1st winter f. *Ad. m.*
DUSKY THRUSH (*ca.* 1/4)

p. 103

Ad. m. spring *Ad. f.* *1st winter m.*
BLACK-THROATED THRUSH (*ca.* 1/4)

p. 104 & p. 101

Ad. f. *Ad. m.* *Ad.*
AMERICAN ROBIN (*ca.* 1/4) GREY-CHEEKED THRUSH

PLATE 29

p. 106 & p. 105

Ad. m. summer *Ad. f. winter* *Ad. winter (upper) Juv. (lower)*
LANCEOLATED WARBLER (1/3) PALLAS'S GRASSHOPPER WARBLER

p. 106

Ad. f. *Ad. m.* *Ad. m.*
SAVI'S WARBLER (1/3)

p. 108

Ad. m. summer *F. winter* *Ad. m.*
MOUSTACHED WARBLER (1/3) CETTI'S WARBLER

p. 109
&
p. 110

Ad. winter *Ad. summer* *Ad. winter* *Ad. m. summer*
PADDYFIELD WARBLER (1/3) BLYTH'S REED WARBLER

p. 126
&
p. 111

Ad. *Ad.*
BONELLI'S WARBLER (*ca.* 2/5) THICK-BILLED WARBLER

p. 114
115
&
p. 113

Ad. m. summer *Ad. m. summer* *Ad. m. summer*
BOOTED WARBLER MELODIOUS WARBLER (1/3)
OLIVACEOUS WARBLER (*lower*)

Ad. m. summer. *Ad. f. summer* *Juv. m.* *F. 1st winter*
SUBALPINE WARBLER (1/3)

p. 117

Juv. m. *Ad. f. (lower)* *Ad. m. (upper)*
SARDINIAN WARBLER (1/3)

p. 118

Ad. f. summer *Ad. m. summer* *Juv.*
ORPHEAN WARBLER (1/3)

p. 119

p. 122
&
p. 121

Autumn *Summer*
ARCTIC WARBLER (*ca.* 1/3) GREENISH WARBLER

p. 124

Ad. f. *Ad. m.* Yellow-browed *(upper)* *Ad. m.* Pallas *(lower)*
YELLOW-BROWED WARBLER PALLAS'S WARBLER (1/3)

p. 125

M. winter (upper) *Ad. m. summer(lower)* *Ad. m. summer* *M. winter (upper)*
DUSKY WARBLER (1/3) RADDE'S WARBLER

p. 127

Ad. m. summer *Ad. f.* *Imm. m.*
COLLARED FLYCATCHER (1/3)

p. 128

Ad. m. winter *Imm. f.*
ISABELLINE SHRIKE (*ca.* 2/5)

p. 129
&
p. 132

Ad. *Ad. m.* *F.*
RED-EYED VIREO (*ca.* 1/3) BLACK-AND-WHITE WARBLER

p. 130

Ad. m. winter (upper) *Ad. f. summer* *Ad. m. summer* *Juv. m.*
CITRIL FINCH (*ca.* 1/3)

p. 133

Ad. m. winter (upper) *Imm. m. (upper)*
Ad. m. summer (lower) *F. (lower)*
YELLOW-RUMPED WARBLER (*ca.* 2/5)

p. 134

Imm. *Ad.*
NORTHERN WATERTHRUSH (*ca.* 1/3)

p. 135

F. *Ad. m. winter* *Juv. m.* *Ad. m. summer*
YELLOWTHROAT (*ca.* 1/2)

Ad. f. *Moulting m.* *Ad. m.*
SUMMER TANAGER (*ca.* 1/3)

p. 136

Imm. *Ad.*
WHITE-THROATED SPARROW (*ca.* 1/3)

p. 137

p. 138

Ad. m. summer *Ad. f.* *Ad. m. winter*
PINE BUNTING (*ca.* 1/3)

p. 139

Ad. f. *Ad. m.*
ROCK BUNTING (1/3)

p. 140

Ad. f. *Ad. m. summer*
YELLOW-BREASTED BUNTING ($^1/_3$)

p. 141

Ad. m. summer *Ad. f.*
RED-HEADED BUNTING ($^1/_3$)

p. 142

Ad. m. summer *Ad. m. winter* *Ad. f.*
ROSE-BREASTED GROSBEAK (*ca* 1/4)

p. 143

Imm. m. *Ad. m.* *Ad. f.*
NORTHERN ORIOLE (*ca.* 1/3)

RED-NECKED NIGHTJAR—*Caprimulgus ruficollis*

PLATE 21

It resembles Nightjar in shape and plumage pattern but is distinguished by its slightly larger size, *yellow-rufous collar*, and a *larger white patch on the throat*. This last feature, though sometimes a useful character, is variable in extent and can be very difficult to ascertain in flight. On wing, however, the bird appears *distinctly bigger and a little redder* than Nightjar, with a more deliberate flight, while *the white wing and tail marks are more conspicuous and present in both sexes*. Its *unmistakable song*, clearly audible at half a mile, draws attention to its presence at night in breeding areas. Length about 12 ins. (30–31 cms.).

Habitat. It has been described as often inhabiting more open country than Nightjar, with scanty vegetation and bushes, but in southern Spain the reverse seems normally to be the case. There it is found chiefly in the pine forests: indeed where small pine-woods are split up by open country it is found almost exclusively among the trees although sometimes in treeless areas of denser ground vegetation (tree-heath, bracken, bramble, etc.).

General Habits. It is crepuscular and nocturnal like the Nightjar. It perhaps perches less frequently in trees, but adopts the same lengthways posture along a branch. Song may be uttered from a tree or from the ground. If flushed by day it generally settles again on the ground quite close at hand.

Song is a very resonant loud "cut-ock", repeated rapidly in long bursts (at a rate of up to 100 calls per minute).

Food consists of insects taken chiefly on the wing, but also from the ground after a short hover and a quick drop.

Status and Distribution. England—One.

Shot Killingworth, near Newcastle, Northumberland, Oct. 5, 1856.

The race concerned, *Caprimulgus ruficollis desertorum*, breeds in N. Africa, and another race occurs in Spain and Portugal. They winter south of Sahara.

1959–1978 No additional records

EGYPTIAN NIGHTJAR—*Caprimulgus aegyptius*

PLATE 21

Colour is *much paler and sandier than the common Nightjar*, and the white in the primaries (a series of white notches on inner webs) is conspicuous in flight; it has no white spots on the wing or tail or black streaks on the back. Length about 10 ins. (25–26 cms.).

Habitat. It is confined to desert and semi-desert regions.

General Habits. Habits are much as Nightjar, but it seems to be more addicted to flocking in Egypt than common Nightjar.

It makes an indistinct snapping sound when flushed.

Food is insects.

Status and Distribution. England—One.

Rainworth, near Mansfield, Notts., June 23, 1883.

The species breeds in N. and N.E. Africa, and in Asia from Sinai to Turkistan and Baluchistan, wintering in N.E. Africa. It is uncertain to which race the British record refers.

1959–1978 No additional records

COMMON NIGHTHAWK—*Chordeiles minor*

PLATE 21

It differs from European and other American nightjars in having *longer wings and slightly forked, instead of rounded, tail. A broad white patch across the primaries* is conspicuous in flight; the tail has a narrow white band in male only. It has a more boldly marbled pattern of blackish and whitish or pale buff than European species; the under-parts are barred, and there is a white patch across the throat. It commonly hunts high in the air with a buoyant rather tern-like flight. Length about 9 ins. (23 cms.).

Habitat. It is more a bird of the open than European Nightjar, its natural habitat being open fields, moors, etc. In U.S.A. it now mainly frequents towns, breeding on flat gravel roofs.

General Habits. It is much more diurnal than Nightjar, regularly becoming active earlier in the evening, and indeed is frequently seen on the wing, and even hunts, at all hours of the day. Is rather gregarious.

Note is a nasal "peent".

Food consists of insects.

Status and Distribution. England—Three.

Female, Tresco, Scilly Isles, Sept. 17, 1927.

Two seen St. Agnes, Scilly Isles, Sept. 28, 1957, one bird remaining until Oct. 5.

The race concerned, *Chordeiles minor minor*, breeds in N. America from the Gulf of Mexico north to the tree limit in Canada and Alaska. Other races occur in S.W. Canada and W. and S. parts of U.S.A. The species winters in S. America.

1959–1978 Five additional records

NEEDLE-TAILED SWIFT—*Hirundapus caudacutus*

PLATE 22

The distinguishing characters are its *large size and very short tail*; it has a white chin, brown breast, and white flanks and vent. The *white horseshoe-shaped area on the hinder part of the body below* is diagnostic. Even when it flies close past, the spiny tips to tail-feathers cannot be distinguished. Length about 7½ ins. (19 cms.).

Habitat. Aerial like other swifts, it frequents not only steep rocky localities, but also sometimes plains.

General Habits. When feeding they often fly low over water or just over tree-tops, sometimes in company with swallows and martins; at other times they circle round at great speed at considerable elevation, too high for the colour pattern to be seen, but the short, unforked tail distinguishes them from species of *Apus*. Flight is even more rapid than that of European swifts.

The call is a scream which is apparently seldom heard outside the breeding season.

Food is insects taken on the wing.

Status and Distribution. Great Britain—Three.

One Great Horkesley, Essex, July 8, 1846.

One Ringwood, Hants., July 26 or 27, 1879.

One seen Fair Isle, Shetland, Aug. 6, 1931.

The race concerned, *Hirundapus caudacutus caudacutus*, breeds from E. Siberia to Japan, and winters in Australia and Tasmania. Another race occurs in India.

1959–1978 One additional record. The Fair Isle record of 1931 is no longer accepted

BLUE-CHEEKED BEE-EATER—*Merops superciliosus*

PLATE 22

Similar in size and outline to the common Bee-eater, the Blue-cheeked Bee-eater is predominantly a *bright parrot-green* bird above and below, with *copper-coloured underwing*. The black bill is long and curved. Above the broad black stripe which runs from bill through eye on to the ear-coverts, is a turquoise blue band which extends across the forehead (becoming whitish immediately above the bill); the blue also extends, but rather inconspicuously, below the black eyestripe. The *chin is yellow, becoming copper-coloured on the throat*, without a black lower border. In flight against the sky when the angle of light can make colour of the mantle uncertain, it is best distinguished from the common Bee-eater by lack of that bird's pale yellowish lower back. The Blue-cheeked's rump has a bluish shade. The sexes are similar. Length about 11 ins. (28 cms.).

Habitat. It frequents open country, perching in exposed situations such as bare branches, on wires or even tall reeds; it is partial to the neighbourhood of water.

General Habits. In undulating direct flight and in periods of gliding and wheeling when hawking insects it resembles Bee-eater. At times it hunts from a low stone or the ground, where its short legs and long tail give it a horizontal carriage. It likes to take its prey from below, in an upward glide.

The call, a husky "treeb", has a similarity to that of the Bee-eater, and is similarly frequently uttered on the wing, but is rather harsher and lower-pitched; when known it is a useful distinguishing character.

Food consists of insects caught in flight.

Status and Distribution. England—One.

Seen St. Agnes, Scilly Isles, June 22, 1951.

The species breeds in N. Africa, Asia north to Transcaspia, and Madagascar; western birds winter in tropical Africa. It is not known which race occurred in England.

1959–1978 No additional records, but one St. Mary's, Scilly Isles, July 13, 1921 now accepted

LESSER SHORT-TOED LARK—*Calandrella rufescens*

PLATE 23

It resembles a miniature Skylark rather more than a Short-toed Lark. It is separated from the latter in all plumages by its *distinctly streaked breast* below creamy throat, and marked dark streaks on the flanks, while Short-toed Lark at all ages usually has under-parts unmarked although young birds have a buffish suffusion across the breast and sometimes a few dark streaks. The colour of the *top of head is uniform with mantle*, whereas Short-toed is often russet-capped. Most Lesser Short-toed Larks have upper-parts greyish or earth-brown, and darker than the typical rufous brown of the Short-toed Lark, but both species are rather variable. The Lesser also lacks the dark neck patches which are often visible on Short-toed, and the buffish eye-stripes may extend further forward to meet on the forehead. The outer tail feathers are whitish. Faint double whitish wing-bar, and in flight secondaries show a rather narrow whitish edge. About size of Meadow Pipit, but stockier, much stouter-billed and with shorter tail and legs. It is thus appreciably smaller than Skylark on ground or in the air. Bill horn or greyish, legs yellow-brown. Length about 5½ ins. (14 cms.).

Habitat. A bird of open, rather bare and flat country including desert and steppe. Irish birds have occurred on fields and grazing land with tussocks of longer grass, and on short grass in areas of marsh and salt-marsh.

General Habits. Gregarious outside the breeding season, tamer than Short-toed Lark, often allowing a close approach and not going far when flushed. It moves in a walk, sometimes a quick run, and will crouch close to ground like other larks, but both in open and when behind a tussock will from time to time stretch upright to full height to look around.

Call notes are a rippling "prrit", rather more liquid than the equivalent note of Short-toed Lark, and a clicking "sik". Song is more varied and less disrupted, and song-flight less undulating, than Short-toed's (latter's song-flight consists of steep undulations, which coincide with the delivery of a regularly repeated brief song phrase).

Food is mainly seeds and plant shoots, also a few insects.

Status and Distribution. Ireland—Four records.

Flock of thirty seen Tralee Bay, Kerry, Jan. 4, 1956.

Five seen Great Saltee, Wexford, March 30–31, 1956.

Two seen near Belmullet, Mayo, May 21, 1956.

Five seen Great Saltee, March 22 (and up to 4 till March 25), 1958.

The bird breeds in Europe in S. Spain and S. Russia, across N. Africa from the Atlantic to Egypt, and across central Asia from the Mediterranean and Caspian to Manchuria. It is not known to which of many races the Irish records refer.

1959–1978 No additional records

RED-RUMPED SWALLOW—*Hirundo daurica*

PLATE 23

Outline on the wing is much as Swallow, but it is readily distinguished from below by *absence of gorget*, whole under-parts being pale buffish, and from above by *sandy-buff upper tail-coverts*, which may lead to confusion with House Martin at a distance if the long outer tail-feathers are not made out. At close quarters its proportions appear quite different from Martin, which looks squat compared with Swallow, while Red-rumped Swallow appears more elongated, and the pale buff is seen to shade into chestnut on rump, while the chestnut nape and superciliary stripe, dark streaks on under-parts and absence of white marks on tail afford further characters. Juveniles are browner with the chestnut paler, more buff. Length about 7 ins. (18 cms.).

Habitat. Open country. For nesting it prefers hilly and rocky districts with caves or cliffs, especially near sea or inland waters; also in some districts is common about bridges, buildings, etc.

General Habits. High soaring flight recalls House Martin rather than Swallow, and action is more deliberate than latter, but it is also often seen flying low. It often associates with both Swallows and Martins. Other habits are much as Swallow.

Flight-note is a sparrow-like chirp; song is slower and more staccato than Swallow's.

Food is insects taken on the wing.

Status and Distribution. British Isles—Seven (but the 1952 records could refer to the same bird).

One shot and two others seen Fair Isle, Shetland, June 2, 1906.

One seen Aldbury, Herts., June 11, 1949.
One seen Cley and Blakeney, Norfolk, March 6–25, 1952.
One seen Lundy, Devon, March 27, 1952.
One seen Great Saltee, Wexford, April 10–11, 1952.

The race concerned, *Hirundo daurica rufula*, breeds from S. Iberian peninsula and N. Africa to the Balkans and Middle East south to Dead Sea and east to Baluchistan, wintering in E. Africa. Other races occur in Asia east to Japan and south to Malaya.

1959–1978 54 additional records

PECHORA PIPIT—*Anthus gustavi*

Plate 24

It has the general colour, build and "stance" of Tree Pipit, but is distinguished by *note* and *two pale streaks down the back*, usually distinct in birds seen in Fair Isle, but not always so. (Moreover other pipits can show buff lines on back at times.) The rump is boldly streaked like Red-throated Pipit's. Underparts are boldly streaked, and outer tail-feathers buffish, not pure white. On passage the note is the best field character as it is very hard to obtain a view of the bird settled anywhere in the open, the bird looking small and dark in the air. Length about 5¾ ins. (14·5 cms.).

Habitat. In the breeding season it frequents swampy ground overgrown with dwarf willow scrub, especially near river-estuaries. On migration on Fair Isle it keeps closely to cover among vegetables, etc.

General Habits. On Fair Isle it skulks and is difficult to flush, while Tree Pipit seldom seeks cover and is easy to flush; Tree Pipit frequently sits on high posts, Pechora Pipit seldom if ever. On the breeding ground, however, it perches freely on trees.

Call-note when flushed is a strong, hard, clear "pwit" given once or more usually repeated several times. It is unlike that of any other British pipit, is lower than Meadow Pipit's call and lacks sweetness of tone. Song is described as very striking, consists of two parts, first a trill, compared to Temminck's Stint or Wood Warbler, and then a low, guttural warble, delivered in song-flight or from perch.

Food consists of insects.

Status and Distribution. Scotland—About fifteen.

All have occurred on Fair Isle, Shetland, mainly in September and October but one late August and one November 19.

The species breeds in N.E. Europe in lower Pechora valley, also in river valleys in Siberia east to Bering Sea; it winters in S.E. Asia. There are no subspecies.

1959–1978 Nine additional records

CITRINE WAGTAIL—*Motacilla citreola*

PLATE 24

It resembles a Yellow Wagtail in front view but from behind resembles a White Wagtail. The male in summer plumage has *head, foreneck and under-parts bright yellow*, greyer on the flanks; a narrow *black collar; back ashy-grey*, darker on the rump; the tail with white on outer feathers; a prominent double white wing-bar. The female at all seasons, and the male in winter, have the crown and nape ashy-grey like the back, while the yellow on forehead, eye-stripe, and under-parts is dulled. In autumn great care must be taken in separating immature Citrine Wagtail from immature Yellow Wagtails, particularly of the Grey-headed race. Young Citrine Wagtail however is a distinct grey on the back (where *flava* have a brownish or greenish tinge); has striking white wing-bars (rather less distinct and yellowish in *flava*); crown grey but *forehead buffish* (instead of grey forehead uniform with crown), ear-coverts grey (not brown); flanks greyish (not olivaceous). At all ages a feature of value in the hand is a white wedge on the basal half of the secondaries and inner primaries. Length about 6½ ins. (16·5 cms.).

Habitat. The Fair Isle birds fed on short grass, a beach and in a marshy area including drainage ditches. The species frequents the same types of country as, and often occurs among, Yellow Wagtails.

General Habits. More sedate than other wagtails, with less movement of tail and head.

The note, a slurred monosyllabic "sweep", is said to be separable from that of Yellow Wagtail, being less shrill and drawn out.

Food is mainly insects, but very little recorded.

Status and Distribution. Scotland—Two.

Immature seen and trapped Fair Isle, Shetland, Sept. 20–24, 1954.

Immature seen and trapped Fair Isle, Oct. 1–5, 1954.

The species breeds from N. and central Russia and Persia east to S.E. Mongolia and central Siberia; it winters in S. Asia. It is not known to which race the British records refer.

1959–1978 24 additional records

RUFOUS BUSH ROBIN—*Cercotrichas galactotes*

PLATE 25

The rather large size, *reddish-brown upper-parts* (greyer in the case of birds from E. Europe, Asia Minor, etc.) and striking tail pattern are unmistakable. Central feathers of the fan-shaped tail are chestnut, but the rest have *broad white tips and black sub-terminal bars*, concealed when the tail closed, but constantly displayed by spreading of the feathers, and conspicuous in flight. The under-parts are buff; there is a white superciliary stripe and a dark mark through the eye. The sexes are similar; young as adults, but with upper-parts paler. Length about 6 ins. (15 cms.).

Habitat. In breeding season it occurs in gardens, vineyards, and other cultivation, and dry, bush-covered localities. It winters chiefly in scrub and thorn-bush country.

General Habits. It frequents both low cover and trees, and is much less skulking than most warblers, perching freely in exposed situations, and frequently hopping about on the ground in the open, with rather upright carriage and tail cocked well up. When perched the tail is constantly spread and moved up and down, while the wings may be drooped and given a forward flick at the same time.

Usual note is a hard "teck, teck". Song is somewhat disjointed, composed of short phrases of clear, lark-like notes.

Food is chiefly insects, also earth-worms.

Status and Distribution. British Isles—Six.

One near Brighton, Sussex, Sept. 16, 1854.

One Start, Devon, Sept. 25, 1859.

One Old Head of Kinsale, Cork, Sept. 1876.

One Slapton, Devon, Oct. 12, 1876.

One seen Great Saltee, Wexford, Sept. 22—Oct. 4, 1951.

One seen Wicks, Dungeness, on the Kent/Sussex border, Sept. 12, 1951.

The first four of the above records refer to the race *Cercotrichas galactotes galactotes* which breeds in Portugal, S. and E. Spain, in N. Africa from Morocco to Egypt, and in Palestine and S. Syria. The bird seen on Great Saltee was considered to belong to one of the greyer races which occur in S.E. Europe, Asia Minor, etc. (*C. g. syriacus*), and from Iraq to Baluchistan (*C. g. famialiaris*); another race occurs in the upper Nile area. The bird winters in Africa, S. Arabia and India.

1959–1978 Four additional records

THRUSH NIGHTINGALE—*Luscinia luscinia*

PLATE 25

Appearance is the same as Nightingale's but under exceptional conditions at close quarters the markings on the breast, giving an effect of *indistinct vertical striations*, might be distinguished. In most cases the greyer and darker shade of the mantle, lacking the rufous of Nightingale, may also be helpful, while in particular the *rump has the same earthy grey shade as the mantle* whereas the rump of Nightingale approaches the rufous of the tail in colour. Very seldom, however, can so skulking a bird be recognized with certainty in the field, and it must be borne in mind that some examples of Thrush Nightingale have rather warm upper-parts and very indistinct striations on the breast; these are probably inseparable in the field from Nightingale. The differences in wing-formula are shown in the drawing opposite. Length about 6½ ins. (16·5 cms.).

Habitat. In the breeding season it haunts exclusively damp deciduous woods and copses with patches of thick undergrowth, and swampy thickets. In winter quarters, dense bush and luxuriant vegetation.

General Habits. Behaviour is like Nightingale, but it is even more partial to damp places.

Call note, "whit", resembles Nightingale's but is sharper and higher-pitched, as is also the croaking note. Song, which might be heard here from a bird on spring passage, is of the same general character as Nightingale's, but lacks its "crescendo" and variety.

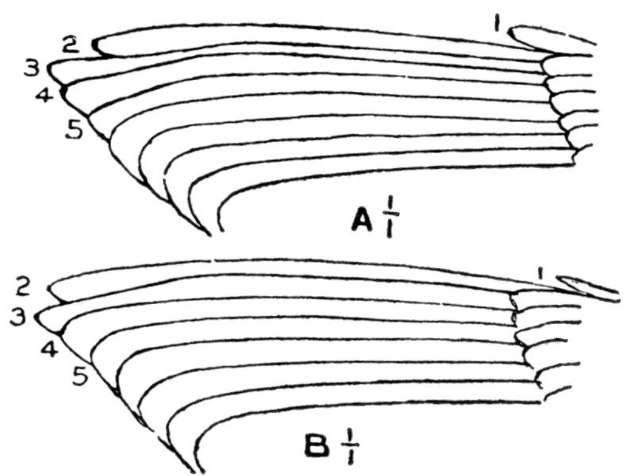

A. The Nightingale (*Luscinia megarhynchos*). B. The Thrush Nightingale (*L. luscinia*). Showing differences in wing-formula. Note especially lengths of 1st and 2nd primaries, and 3rd and 4th emarginated in Nightingale and only 3rd in Thrush Nightingale.

Food is chiefly worms and larvae of insects. Berries are also eaten.

Status and Distribution. Scotland—Three.

One Fair Isle, Shetland, May 15, 1911.

One trapped Fair Isle, May 10, 1957.

One seen and trapped Fair Isle, May 15–17, 1958.

The species breeds from S. Scandinavia and Austria eastwards to S.W. Siberia and Semipalatinsk; it winters in E. Africa and S. Arabia. There are no subspecies.

1959–1978 37 additional records

RED-FLANKED BLUETAIL—*Tarsiger cyanurus*

PLATE 25

In size and shape resembling a Redstart, the adult male is very distinctive with *blue upper-parts, bright orange-rufous flanks,* and the rest of the under-parts creamy white with a tinge of buff on the breast; the upper-parts and sides of neck are mainly dark blue but the rump and tail are bright cobalt as is line curving over the eye, and forehead is sometimes white. In the female the upper-parts and wings are olive brown, but the rump and tail are dull blue; the under-parts are greyish-white, browner on the breast, but flanks are rufous as in male. Juveniles are heavily spotted like young Robins. Males apparently take 2 years to attain full adult plumage, and may be found breeding in immature plumage resembling that of female; intermediate coloration also occurs. In the field the red flanks are often more evident than the blue in the plumage, and the white of the throat contrasts sharply with the dark cheeks and side of neck. Length about 5½ ins. (14 cms.).

Habitat. In the breeding season it frequents old woodland with an abundance of decaying logs, both spruce mixed with birch on hill slopes with rocky outcrops, and tall dense spruce forest, often damp. In either case it seems that the male may seek a singing post with an open view such as provided by the top of an outstandingly tall tree, a hill slope, edge of a lake or other open place. On passage it visits gardens as well as more wooded country.

General Habits. A shy bird in its breeding quarters, the singing male when disturbed diving into cover very readily. In winter quarters it is more confiding and robin-like, flitting or feeding along tracks, seeking insects low in trees or bushes or on ground, also hawking like a flycatcher. Song is short, clear, striking and far-carrying, somewhat reminiscent of a thrush, "tiil-tyle, tiil-tyle" preceded and followed by some quieter notes. The call is a short "teck-teck", rather robin-like. Alarm note is a grating sound like a small clock being wound up.

Food appears chiefly to consist of insects, especially beetles and larvae. Spiders also recorded. Berries are taken in autumn.

Status and Distribution. Great Britain—Three.

One seen North Cotes, Lincs., September 1903.

One shot Whalsay, Shetland, Oct. 7, 1947.

Immature male found dead Sandwich, Kent, Oct. 28, 1956.

The race concerned, *Tarsiger cyanurus cyanurus*, breeds from Finland (probably), across north-central Asia to Japan. Other races occur from Kashmir to central China. The bird winters south to Indo-China.

1959–1978 Five additional records

ISABELLINE WHEATEAR—*Oenanthe isabellina*

PLATE 26

The sexes are similar, suggesting females of other species of wheatear. *Large size and uniform pale sandy appearance* are distinctive. Some very pale females or young males of Greenland race of common Wheatear might easily be mistaken for Isabelline, but latter has a considerably broader black band across tail. The large bill and big-headed appearance of the Isabelline are noticeable in the field. Length about 6½ ins. (16·5 cms.).

Habitat. In the breeding season it haunts steppe or desert country and barren tracts on plains or lower slopes of hills. In winter-quarters it shows preference for open sandy places.

General Habits. Behaviour is as other wheatears. It perches as much on bushes as on the ground.

Call is a loud "cheep" and a whistling "wheet, whit".

Food is probably chiefly insects, and some seeds. Lizard also recorded.

Status and Distribution. England—One.

Female Allonby, Cumberland, Nov. 11, 1887.

The species breeds from S.E. Russia south to Jordan and east to Baluchistan, and winters in N.E. Africa and S.W. Asia. There are no subspecies.

1959–1978 One additional record

PIED WHEATEAR—*Oenanthe pleschanka*

PLATE 26

The black back of male distinguishes it from the black-throated phase of the eastern race of Black-eared Wheatear, which it otherwise resembles. The tail pattern approximately resembles that of Wheatear but has more black on outer feathers. *Under-parts are buff.* It requires also to be distinguished from three other black-backed and black-throated Palearctic Wheatears (not on British list): Red-rumped (*Oenanthe moesta*), Hooded (*Oenanthe monacha*) and Mourning (*Oenanthe lugens*). But all these have white under-parts, while the Red-rumped is considerably bigger with little or no white in the tail which is often rufous; Hooded lacks the black band across the end of the tail which is mainly white apart from the black central pair of feathers, has a larger bill, and a greater expanse of black on breast; Mourning has much white on inner webs of primaries visible in flight, buff under tail-coverts, and tail pattern approximately as that of Wheatear. The female has light brownish grey upper-parts, a fairly dark buff pectoral band, and under-parts almost white. In worn summer plumage, it is very difficult to separate in the field from the female of the eastern race of Black-eared Wheatear, although typically the Pied is then greyer earth-brown above and has a better defined pectoral band; in fresh autumn plumage the best field character is the prominence of the contrasting pale fringes of the mantle feathers, which are absent in Black-eared. The tail pattern of both birds is similar. Length about 5¾ ins. (14·5 cms.).

Habitat. It nests on stony slopes and broken ground with scanty vegetation. Haunts in winter quarters are varied: stony ground on plains or hills, also about habitations and gardens.

General Habits. Although usually haunting stony places, it frequently perches on bushes and trees, often high up on the latter. It constantly pounces down on to the ground and flies up again to its perch in a shrike-like fashion, and does not normally hop on ground searching for food like Wheatear. Continually "bobs" its tail, and is very shy and equally conspicuous when breeding, but the Dorset bird was remarkably fearless. It lacked the upright stance of Wheatear.

Note is a harsh "zack, zack", resembling Wheatear.

Food is chiefly insects and some seeds.

Status and Distribution. Great Britain—Three.
Female, Isle of May, Fife, Oct. 19, 1909.
Female Swona, Orkney, Nov. 1, 1916.
Female seen and trapped Portland, Dorset, Oct. 17–19, 1954.

The race concerned, *Oenanthe pleschanka pleschanka*, breeds from Roumania across Russia and central Asia east to Mongolia and south to Afghanistan; it winters in N.E. Africa. Another race occurs in Cyprus.

1959–1978 Three additional records

DESERT WHEATEAR—*Oenanthe deserti*

Plate 26

Both sexes differ from other wheatears in having the *tail black almost to the base*, and the wing-coverts show a good deal of whitish. The *black throat of male* distinguishes it at a glance from other species except the black-throated phase of Black-eared Wheatear, browner examples of which (except for tail) it much resembles, but it has scapulars as mantle, not black like the wing as in Black-eared. Rump and upper tail-coverts are white, but more or less tinged buff, especially in female; underparts buff. Female has a whitish throat, but may show some black in summer. Autumn males, especially young, have white fringes to the throat feathers. An adult male wintering on Yorkshire moorland had all colours dulled; two panels of dull white, roughly oblong in shape, were the most conspicuous feature of the closed wing, and in flight they superficially resembled the markings on a Chaffinch's wing. Length about 5¾ ins. (14·5 cms.).

Habitat. It frequents barren and rocky or sandy wastes with thin scrubby vegetation; also, in winter, cultivation where this is interspersed with barren patches.

General Habits. Behaviour is as common Wheatear. It is rather silent, appearing for a moment and taking a short flight before again showing itself. It perches freely on small desert bushes and seems to prefer them to rocks when both are available; also recorded perching in trees.

Call note is rather plaintive, hoarse whistle.

Food is normally insects and a few seeds.

Status and Distribution. Great Britain—Twelve.

Male near Alloa, Clackmannan, Nov. 26, 1880.

Female Holderness coast, Yorks., Oct. 17, 1885.

Male near Arbroath, Angus, Dec. 28, 1887.

Male Pentland Skerries, Orkney, June 2, 1906.

Male Norfolk coast, Oct. 31, 1907.

Male Fair Isle, Shetland, Oct. 6, 1928.

Male Fair Isle, Oct. 26, 1929.

Immature male Fair Isle, Nov. 18, 1940.

One seen and trapped near Halifax, Yorks., Nov. 12, 1949 to Jan. 22, 1950.

Female seen Marazion Marsh, Cornwall, Aug. 29, 1950.

Male seen and trapped Jarrow Slake, Durham, Dec. 4–18, 1955.

Male seen East Mersea, Essex, Jan. 12–13 and Feb. 3, 1958.

Most of the above birds were not identified subspecifically but they include examples of *Oenanthe deserti deserti* (1906, 1928) and *Oenanthe deserti homochroa* (1885, 1907, 1929). The first-named race breeds from the Nile eastwards across central Asia to Mongolia; the latter, the western race, from the Nile westwards across N. Africa to Morocco; another race occurs in Tibet. The species winters in Africa and in Asia from Arabia to India.

1959–1978 Nine additional records

BLACK WHEATEAR—*Oenanthe leucura*

PLATE 26

The black plumage, with white rump and under tail-coverts and regular wheatear tail pattern make it unmistakable at all ages; it is also appreciably *larger* and bulkier than common Wheatear. Females, and still more juveniles, are a duller, browner black than male. Length about 7 ins. (18 cms.).

Habitat. It frequents cliffs, gorges and rocky or boulder-strewn places, chiefly in mountains, or semi-desert.

General Habits. Behaviour is like other wheatears. Often rather shy. It will perch on trees and bushes where present.

Song is a brief, pleasing warble with a mellowness comparable to Blue Rock Thrush or Orphean Warbler; it is often given on the wing and is commonly introduced and terminated by a sibilant churring. Alarm note is a piping "pee-pee-pee-pee", sometimes followed by a single or double slurred "chack".

Food consists mainly of insects.

Status and Distribution. Great Britain—Four.

One seen Fair Isle, Shetland, Sept. 28–30, 1912.

One seen Altrincham, Cheshire, Aug. 1, 1943.

One seen Fair Isle, Oct. 19, 1953.

One seen Dungeness, Kent, Oct. 17, 1954.

The typical race breeds in the Mediterranean region of W. Europe from Italy to Portugal; other races occur in N. Africa. It is not known to which race the British records refer.

1959–1978 One additional record

ROCK THRUSH—*Monticola saxatilis*

PLATE 27

A rather plump bird of Song Thrush size but with a shorter, *orange tail* (central feathers brown), which is diagnostic at all ages. This with the *blue head, white patch on back, orange under-parts* and blackish wings, make the male in the breeding season equally unmistakable at rest or in flight. In winter plumage the colours are more or less obscured by brown tips to feathers above and whitish below. Female is mottled dark brown above, without or with scarcely any white, and beneath is more or less rufous buff, with dark crescentic markings. Young in late summer are paler and more strongly marked than female, rather "washed-out" looking, but always with the characteristic tail. Length about 7½ ins. (19 cms.).

Habitat. It nests in rocky ground, with or without scattered trees, or in vicinity of ruins, ordinarily at high altitudes in mountains. In winter quarters it is found in savanna country.

General Habits. The short tail, frequently upright carriage (though a rather crouching attitude is also common), and to a great extent behaviour, suggest a chat more than a thrush. Spends most of its time on the ground, moving with long hops, perching on rocks and boulders, though also on trees and buildings, and even telegraph-wires. It usually flies low and is shy and wary, ready to dive behind a boulder or disappear round a hill-face. Has a characteristic flirting action of tail. The male has a zooming and diving song-flight in spring.

Ordinary note "chack, chack" recalls Blackbird's, but is softer.

Food is insects of all kinds; also lizards, spiders, molluscs, frogs, worms and berries of various kinds.

Status and Distribution. Great Britain—Six.

One Therfield, Herts., May 19, 1843.

Male obtained and another seen Pentland Skerries, Orkney, May 17, 1910.

One Fair Isle, Shetland, Nov. 8, 1931.

One seen Dungeness, Kent, June 23, 1933.

Male seen Fair Isle, Oct. 16–17, 1936.

The species breeds from central Europe south to the Mediterranean, also N.W. Africa, and across central Asia to China; it winters in tropical Africa. There are no subspecies.

1959–1978 Six additional records

SIBERIAN THRUSH—*Zoothera sibirica*

PLATE 27

The male is most distinctive, at rest appearing *almost uniform slate black, but with a long, outstandingly white eye-stripe*. The outer tail feathers are deeply tipped white (more visible from below than above), under-tail coverts are marked with white crescents, and the belly is whitish; none of these features is readily noticeable on the ground. In flight *a broad white band running obliquely almost the whole length of the underwing* is conspicuous, and there is a shorter narrower white underwing band near the wing root, while a row of clear white spots appears across the end of the tail. The body colour has a bluish tinge, with a paler patch on the flanks, and crown blacker. The head has a flat, not rounded, appearance owing to shallow forehead and flat skull. The female is rather like a Song Thrush: upper parts are brown with a slight olive tinge; sides and front of neck paler and spotted; rest of under-parts whitish broadly barred with slightly crescentic brownish marks; it has a buffish eye-stripe. Like male, it has the outer tail feathers tipped with white, and has a similar characteristic underwing pattern, but the broad oblique bar is yellowish. The juvenile is more spotted than the female. Length about 9 ins. (23 cms.).

Underwing of Siberian Thrush (*Zoothera sibirica*).

Habitat. A cover-loving bird, frequenting mainly the parts of thickets and forests which border on water; it is also encountered in the alpine birch zone.

General Habits. Normally very shy. The behaviour of the bird on the Isle of May most resembled a Blackbird; while not unduly shy it tended to skulk under huts and other cover. Its calls were recorded as a short "zit", similar to but a little softer than that of Song Thrush, and a gruff squawk when flushed suddenly; in general it was rather silent. On the breeding ground the song is monotonous but sonorous and consists of a disyllabic flute-like whistle and a quiet chattering.

Food consists mainly of worms and other animal matter.

Status and Distribution. Scotland—One.

Adult male trapped Isle of May, Fife, October 2, 1954.

The species breeds from central Siberia to Japan, and winters in S.E. Asia. It is not certain to which race the British record refers.

1959–1978 Two additional records

SWAINSON'S THRUSH (or OLIVE-BACKED THRUSH)—*Catharus ustulatus*

PLATE 27

This small American thrush is uniform olive brown or grey-brown above, pale below and spotted with black on upper breast and sides of throat. The sides of the head, throat and upper breast are washed buff, and there is a conspicuous buff eye-ring. It can only be separated from the Grey-cheeked Thrush in a view sufficiently close and clear to see the *buff cheeks and throat, and the broader buff eye-ring* of Swainson's. The uniform olive or greyish upper-parts of both species distinguish them from other common American thrushes, i.e. Wood Thrush (*Hylocichla mustelina*) which is more rufous on the head and more olivaceous towards the tail, the Hermit Thrush (*Catharus guttatus*) which is olivaceous on the head and more rufous towards the tail, and the upper-parts of the Veery (*Catharus fuscescens*) which are uniformly more or less rufous. Swainson's Thrush has a blackish bill and pale brownish legs. Length about 7 ins. (18 cms.).

Habitat. It nests chiefly in spruce and fir forests, especially the damper sections. On passage it occurs in open woodland glades, copses and cover along roads, streams, and in parks and gardens, as well as deep forest.

General Habits. Although shy and retiring like other thrushes of this group, it is not infrequently seen in tree-tops. It feeds in the foliage, on the ground and to a lesser extent by fly-catching. In cover it will at times remain motionless to avoid detection.

The usual note is a weak, high-pitched "pip" or "whit". Song is often heard on spring passage, the musical throaty phrases tending to rise in pitch.

Food is mainly insects, with some spiders, snails and worms. Vegetable food includes fruits, berries and seeds.

Status and Distribution. Ireland—One.

Found dead Blackrock Lighthouse, Mayo, May 26, 1956.

The race concerned, *Catharus ustulatus swainsoni*, breeds from north-central Canada to West Virginia. The species breeds from Alaska to Newfoundland, and south to West Virginia and California; it winters from S. Mexico to Peru and Argentine.

1959–1978 Three additional records

GREY-CHEEKED THRUSH—*Catharus minimus*

PLATES 27 and 28

A small thrush with greyish brown back, very similar to Swainson's Thrush from which it is only distinguishable by its *grey cheeks, inconspicuous whitish eye-ring*, colder coloured throat and breast, and greyer back. These points are usually detected easily in a good view, but a few individuals in autumn may be barely separable except by call-notes. Both species are smaller than Song Thrush, with darker upper-parts, and apart from the spotted throat and upper breast (less buff-washed in Grey-cheeked than in Swainson's), their under-parts and particularly the flanks are a much clearer, colder grey-white, lacking the distinct spotting and buff colouring of the Song Thrush. Length about 7¾ ins. (19·5–20 cms.).

Habitat. Nests in northern willow and birch scrub, and stunted spruce. On migration it occurs in damp woodlands, road- and stream-side thickets, and garden shrubberies, keeping usually near the ground.

General Habits. A shy, retiring bird at all seasons, seldom perching high or in the open except when in song, and slipping into undergrowth when disturbed. Migrants are often seen feeding in leaf-litter on the ground, hopping with erect carriage. Active in the evening and early morning on the nesting grounds.

The usual note "quee-a" or "wheu" is down-slurred, nasal and longer than the quite different brief "whit" of Swainson's Thrush. Weak thin song is sometimes heard from spring migrants.

Food is chiefly insects including beetles, ants, wasps, bees, caterpillars, also a few grasshoppers, worms, spiders, crawfish. Wild berries and fruits are of importance particularly in autumn.

Status and Distribution. Scotland—Two.

One trapped Fair Isle, Shetland, Oct. 5, 1953.

One trapped Fair Isle, Oct. 29, 1958.

The species breeds from Newfoundland across Canada to Alaska and south to north-east U.S.A.; it also breeds in N.E. Siberia. It winters in north-western S. America. It is not known to which race the British records refer.

1959–1978 11 additional records

DUSKY THRUSH—*Turdus eunomus*

PLATE 28

The *broad whitish eye-stripe* renders confusion unlikely with anything but Redwing and non-British Naumann's Thrush (*T. naumanni*) amongst European species. It differs from the former in having chestnut on the coverts and secondaries, also a blackish breast and flanks in summer, much obscured, however, by white edgings in winter, producing a more spotted effect below; while Naumann's Thrush has the black replaced by chestnut, and is more or less chestnut in the tail. The upper-parts are blackish-brown, usually more or less mottled chestnut, especially on the rump; throat is whitish with spots at sides; under-wing inconspicuously chestnut. Females and young in autumn are duller and browner, with less chestnut on the wing. A bird seen in winter had the long eye-stripes extending onto sides of nape, mantle grey-brown and slightly streaked, the paler rump seldom showed a reddish tinge; a creamy white gorget above a clearly defined breastband of heavy spotting, followed by a narrow whitish band, followed by a second but incomplete dark band. Length about 9 ins. (23 cms.).

Habitat. It nests in outskirts of forest and thinly wooded country; also deciduous coppice and scrub. In winter it prefers open fields and grassland with thin forest.

General Habits. Gregarious in winter; habits much as Fieldfare but tamer; bill normally carried pointing distinctly upwards. Song like Song Thrush's; call a soft chuckle.

Food is worms, insects, seeds and berries.

Status and Distribution. England—One.

Shot near Gunthorpe, Notts., Oct. 13, 1905.

The species breeds in E. Siberia from the River Yenisei to Kamchatka, and winters from N. India to Japan. There are no subspecies.

[Note. This bird is sometimes treated as a race of Naumann's Thrush *Turdus naumanni*.]

1959–1978 Four additional records

BLACK-THROATED THRUSH—*Turdus ruficollis*

PLATE 28

In size, shape and long-proportioned tail, this thrush is very like a Fieldfare. The *extensive black throat*, contrasting sharply with the whitish lower breast and belly, and *uniform grey-brown upper-parts* are distinctive of the male; the crown is rather darker than the mantle. The female has a whitish throat with black streaks, and upper breast more or less closely marked black; it normally lacks the chestnut in the tail which is a feature of the non-British form, the Red-throated Thrush (*Turdus ruficollis ruficollis*). The under-wing is rufous-buff, belly white, flanks streaked grey. Immature birds resemble the female, but males show some approach to adult male colouring. The bill of a mid-winter male was dark brown with the basal two-thirds of lower mandible a striking orange-yellow. Length about 9¼ ins. (23·5 cms.).

Habitat. It nests in borders and open parts of fir forest, more rarely in pine, aspen and birch woods. It prefers glades and clearings to thick woodland. In winter it occurs in India in damp groves and cultivation, but some remain in the breeding area near villages.

General Habits. Habits are much as Fieldfare, flocking in winter, feeding on the ground in the open, and flying up into trees when disturbed; but it can be confiding and reluctant to fly. It elevates its tail on alighting, like a Blackbird.

Ordinary note is not unlike the alarm chuckle of Blackbird, but much softer; another is like Redwing's call.

Food is probably worms, insects and berries.

Status and Distribution. Great Britain—Three.

Male Lewes, Sussex, Dec. 23, 1868.

One near Perth, February 1879.

One seen and trapped Fair Isle, Shetland, Dec. 8, 1957–about Jan. 22, 1958.

The race (or form) concerned, *Turdus ruficollis atrogularis*, breeds from E. Russia east to River Yenisei, and winters from Iraq to N. India. It is replaced in south central Siberia and N. Mongolia by the very distinct red-throated form *Turdus ruficollis ruficollis*.

1959–1978 Six additional records

AMERICAN ROBIN—*Turdus migratorius*

PLATE 28

Apart from coloration it is in many respects the American counterpart of our Blackbird, with some close similarities in size, habits, carriage and notes. The American Robin's main feature is the *brick-red breast*, this colour extending over all the under-parts except on the black-streaked whitish throat, and the lower belly which is buff or whitish. The upper parts are dark grey, with head and tail blackish in male; the outer tail feathers are tipped white, and there is a *conspicuous broken white eye-ring*. The female resembles male but is rather duller below and a little paler above. Juvenile birds are similar but have the breast spotted with black, and back streaked. Albinism is not uncommon. Bill is yellow, legs brownish. Length about 10 ins. (25–26 cms.).

Habitat. In the nesting season it is predominantly associated with civilization, frequenting gardens, orchards and cultivated country generally provided some cover is available, and commonly penetrates towns; it also nests in more naturally wooded country. In autumn and winter it resorts largely to more secluded woodlands, pastures and swamps.

General Habits. Many of its habits resemble the Blackbird's, for example conspicuous summer feeding on lawn and meadow, but it is more nervous and restless with flicking wings and tail, aggressive in the breeding season but becoming furtive and wary in an excitable way in autumn flocks. Dissimilarities include its pronounced migratory behaviour, wildness in winter and communal roosts which are sometimes large even in the breeding season.

Anxiety notes are "seech, each-each-each", and "tut-tut-tut" with jerking of tail. The song is a succession of liquid phrases "cheerily cheery", similar in tone to Blackbird's but less varied.

Food includes a wide range of berries, fruits and seeds, also many insects and considerable quantities of worms.

Status and Distribution. British Isles—Three.

One seen and trapped Lundy Island, Devon, Oct. 27–Nov. 8, 1952.

One seen Camolin, Wexford, mid-December, 1954.

One seen Blennerville, Kerry, Jan. 11–13, 1955.

The species breeds in N. America from Newfoundland to Alaska and south to S. Mexico; it winters from S. Canada south to Guatemala. It is not known to which race the British records refer.

1959–1978 12 additional records. One Devon, October 1955, is now widely accepted; less widely, seven records 1876–1937

PALLAS'S GRASSHOPPER WARBLER—*Locustella certhiola*

PLATE 29

The general plumage of a bird on Fair Isle was much like Grasshopper Warbler, but differed strikingly in the *rufous-brown streaky rump and upper tail-coverts*; more heavily striated effect of crown and mantle; *dark rounded tail* contrasting markedly in flight with rump and mantle and darkening perceptibly towards the tip (occasionally showing greyish-white tips to tail feathers in flight); and tawny-buff of under tail-coverts. It had an indistinct pale eye-stripe, blackish streaks on crown and mantle, but apparently not on the paler, dull yellowish-brown nape. The under-parts, especially throat, are whiter than Sedge or Grasshopper Warbler, generally with fine spots across the breast; in immature birds the under-parts may be almost uniform dull yellowish. Legs pinkish, bill apparently black. Length about 5¼ ins. (13–13·5 cms.).

Habitat. It nests in damp meadows with thick grass and bushes, and ground overgrown with rank plants. In winter quarters it frequents rice-fields, as well as reeds and water-plants in swamps.

General Habits. Habits are much as Grasshopper Warbler and it is very skulking.

Wintering birds have note rendered "chir-chirr".

Food consists of insects.

Status and Distribution. British Isles—Three.

Male Rockabill Lighthouse, Dublin, Sept. 28, 1908.

Immature seen Fair Isle, Shetland, Oct. 8–9, 1949.

Immature trapped Fair Isle, Oct. 2, 1956.

The species breeds from W. Siberia and W. China to Manchuria; it winters in India and S.E. Asia. It is not known to which race the British records refer.

1959–1978 Two additional records

LANCEOLATED WARBLER—*Locustella lanceolata*

PLATE 29

It resembles a small Grasshopper Warbler in shape; the main points of difference of one seen in the field on Fair Isle were the *well-defined gorget* of close, parallel, vertical striations on the breast, the whitish chin and throat, an indistinct buff-white stripe through the eye, and broad dark striations on the mantle. The bill is dark brown above, with a pale flesh lower mandible; legs pink. Length about 4½ ins. (11·5 cms.).

Habitat. It frequents wet meadows and marshy localities with bushes and rank vegetation, and reeds bordering water.

General Habits. Habits are like Grasshopper Warbler. It is very skulking, creeping about in low cover more like a mouse than a bird, and may pay little attention to human beings.

Note in winter is described as "chir-chirrr", similar to Pallas's Grasshopper Warbler, or as a rolling, chuckling note.

Food is probably insects.

Status and Distribution. Great Britain—Nine.
Male North Cotes, Lincs., Nov. 18, 1909.
One Pentland Skerries, Orkney, Oct. 26, 1910.
Seven at Fair Isle, Shetland, as follows:
One Sept. 9, 1908;
One Oct. 24, 1925;
One Sept. 26, 1926;
One Sept. 22, 1928;
One shot Sept. 29, 1938;
One seen May 4, 1953;
One trapped Sept. 21, 1957.

The species breeds from N.E. Russia across Siberia to Japan; it winters from S. China and India to Indonesia. There are no subspecies.

1959–1978 17 additional records

SAVI'S WARBLER—*Locustella luscinioides*

PLATE 29

A soberly-coloured brown bird, darker than, say, a Reed Warbler, which it is not unlike (though with the form of a Grasshopper Warbler) with *strongly graduated tail* and lighter below, palest on throat, but not always white, as sometimes stated. Plumage lacks distinctive features but, at least in the breeding season, *the trilling song* precludes confusion with anything but Grasshopper Warbler and possibly River Warbler (*Locustella fluviatilis*). It is distinguished from the former by *unspotted plumage* and from the latter by absence of throat-streaks as well as different habits, while the trills are also distinguishable. Length about 5½ ins. (14 cms.).

Habitat. In breeding season it haunts reedy swamps and fens, typically where reeds are not too dense and mixed with undergrowth of sedge, rushes, etc., over shallow water; often with scattered sallows or other bushes. In winter quarters it occurs similarly in swamps and reed-beds.

General Habits. It is restless, but in breeding season not shy, ascending dead reed stems to sing in full view. It hops and creeps with remarkable facility and speed through tangle of dead reeds and swamp vegetation; seldom seen away from cover. After the breeding-season it is stated to disperse to some extent into more open fen and swamp outside reed-beds.

It has a scolding-note something like thin "tzwick" or "tzwee". Song is a trill closely resembling Grasshopper Warbler's but rather lower-pitched and fuller and often less prolonged, though recorded up to as much as 162 secs. It is frequently preceded by a sequence of low ticking notes which gather speed and merge into the trill, without counterpart in Grasshopper Warbler.

Food is mainly insects.

Status and Distribution. Great Britain—Until about the middle of the nineteenth century it was a regular summer visitor breeding in small numbers in East Anglia. Since 1885 records are:

One shot and another seen Fair Isle, Shetland, May 14, 1908.

One seen Wicken Fen, Cambridge, June 2, to mid-August, 1954.

The race concerned, *Locustella luscinioides luscinioides*, breeds in N. Africa and S. Europe north to Holland and Poland, and east to the Caspian; it winters in N. Africa and the Nile valley. Another race occurs from the Caspian to Semipalatinsk.

1959–1978 Over 200 records; several pairs now breeding in S. and E. England

MOUSTACHED WARBLER—*Acrocephalus melanopogon*

PLATE 29

It closely resembles a dark Sedge Warbler, but the following features help identification: the *crown is black at the sides and only slightly paler in the centre*, where Sedge Warbler's is distinctly paler and greyer; *a chalk-white eye-stripe* (not creamy as in Sedge) which is cut off squarely on the nape (not tapering or merging in colour); the under-parts are mainly white with a yellow suffusion on breast (Sedge Warbler everywhere more cream or buff below); a brighter and more extensive area of rufous on rump; tail smoothly rounded (that of Sedge Warbler more acutely tapering and the curve broken by the longer, pointed central pair of feathers). Finally the Sedge Warbler is generally tawnier above and below, lacking in contrast whereas the darker, more rufous, upper-parts and darker crown of Moustached Warbler contrast markedly with the white eye-stripe and under-parts. However, as Sedge Warbler may be rather variable, the Moustached remains a difficult bird to identify by plumage, but recognition is assisted by distinctive notes in song (assuming they are never imitated by Sedge). Bill and legs are pale brown. Length about 5 ins. (12·75 cms.).

Habitat. It nests in extensive reed-beds in swamps, or on lake borders where an admixture of bushes is available. In winter it may frequent smaller areas of reedy swamp where it does not breed.

General Habits. It is usually seen perched on a reed, but when moving about amongst swamp vegetation cocks its tail at times in a manner quite unlike other *Acrocephalus*, which its habits resemble.

Scolding-note is a Sedge Warbler-like churr. Song is softer than Sedge Warbler's, but includes a phrase like Nightingale's "lu-lu-lu-lu".

Food is probably insects.

Status and Distribution. England—One breeding record and three other occurrences.

A pair feeding three young, Cambridge, Aug. 3, last seen Aug. 20, 1946.

Two seen Totton, Hants., Aug. 13, 1951.

One seen Cliffe, Kent, April 14, 1952.

The species breeds in N. Africa and Mediterranean Europe north to Hungary, also in Asia from N. Arabia to Lake Balkhash; it winters from the Mediterranean region to N.W. India and south to Lake Chad. It is not known to which race the British records refer.

1959–1978 One additional record

PADDYFIELD WARBLER—*Acrocephalus agricola*

PLATE 30

A *prominent cream-coloured eye-stripe* prevents confusion with Reed or Marsh Warbler; its *pale coloration*, sandy buff below and reddish brown above, is thought to be responsible for the surprisingly large appearance of a bird on Fair Isle, which in some respects looked like a pale, almost sandy, Reed Warbler. The tail is fairly long, and rounded. In the hand the colour of the upper-parts is much as Reed Warbler and not so olivaceous as Marsh Warbler; it differs from both in the wing being shorter, the 2nd primary is shorter (between 6th and 7th instead of 4th and 5th), the 3rd to 5th primaries are emarginated instead of 3rd only. It is most like Blyth's Reed Warbler in the primaries but the wing is shorter and upper-parts more rufous. (See sketches of wing-outlines under Blyth's Reed Warbler, p. 110.) Upper mandible blackish, lower pale flesh with brown tip, legs flesh-coloured. Length about 5 ins. (12·75 cms.).

Habitat. It haunts reeds, sedge, willows, rank grass and other waterside or swamp vegetation of all kinds.

General Habits. Cover-loving, its habits are described as very similar to Reed Warbler.

Note is described as "chik-chik".

Food is presumably insects.

Status and Distribution. Scotland—Two.

Male shot Fair Isle, Shetland, Oct. 1, 1925.

One trapped Fair Isle, Sept. 16, 1953.

The race concerned, *Acrocephalus agricola agricola*, breeds in S. Russia and across central Asia to Mongolia; it winters in India. Other races occur in Kashmir, China, Manchuria.

1959–1978 Three additional records

BLYTH'S REED WARBLER—*Acrocephalus dumetorum*

PLATE 30

Although very difficult to separate from Marsh Warbler in the field (except by song) it is a colder and more uniform brown, and has a *noticeably longer beak* than others of this genus. Length about 5 ins. (12·75 cms.).

N.B. Garden Warbler (*Sylvia borin*), which can approach Marsh Warbler in coloration in autumn, also has a notch on inner web of 2nd primary resembling Reed or Marsh Warbler, but Garden Warbler's 1st primary is half to two-thirds as long as primary coverts. Occasionally a Garden Warbler has slight emargination on the 3rd and 4th primaries as in Blyth's Reed Warbler.

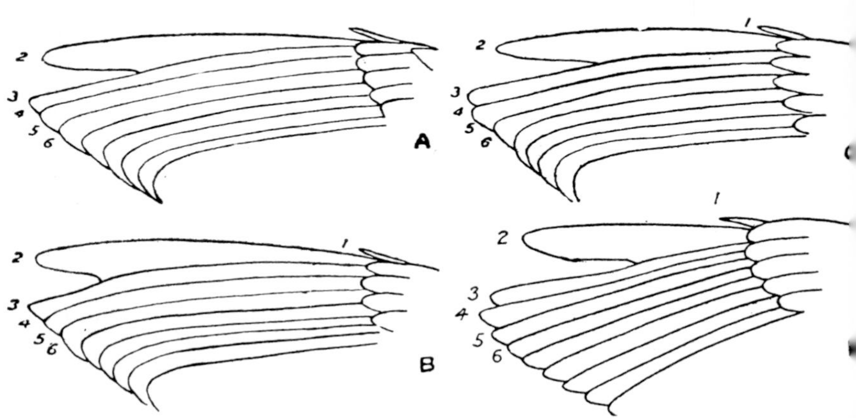

A. Reed Warbler (*A. scirpaceus*). B. Marsh Warbler (*A. palustris*). C. Blyth's Reed Warbler (*A. dumetorum*). D. Paddyfield Warbler (*A. agricola*). Note differences in relative length of 2nd primaries and position of notch on inner web of this primary.

Habitat. It nests in much the same places as Marsh Warbler; not only willow, etc., but also wild gardens and other places with trees and bushes on dry ground. It occupies similar habitats in winter.

General Habits. Habits are similar, but it is more arboreal; at least in winter-quarters and on migration it is often found in foliage of tall trees, hedges or scrub, and may emerge onto exposed sprays of the latter. It has also been compared to a leaf-warbler in habits.

Like Marsh Warbler it is an excellent mimic; it usually sings 2–5 ft. above the ground, mainly at night in the north, and the singing bird can be approached very closely. Blyth's is the louder singer of the two, but with even strength and tempo running on smoothly for long periods. Marsh Warbler on the other hand has a variable tempo, repeating a mimicked phrase rather faster than Blyth's, then switching into very fast, fervent and fluent song, before a sudden stop to begin another more peaceful imitation. Some song is heard in winter quarters. Call notes are described as a sharp "tchik, tchik" and a rather sparrow-like "chrrr", but the Holy Island example had a double note, "tup, tup" something like alarm of Lesser Whitethroat, but much softer and less harsh, unlike any Reed Warbler note.

Food is presumably insects.

Status and Distribution. Great Britain—Nine or ten.

One Fair Isle, Shetland, Sept. 29–30, 1910.

One Spurn Point, Yorks., Sept. 20, 1912.

One Holy Island, Northumberland, Sept. 25, 1912.

Four or five single birds Fair Isle, Sept. 24–Oct. 1, 1912.

One Dudgeon Lightship, Norfolk, Oct. 20–21, 1912.

One Fair Isle, Sept. 24, 1928.

The species breeds from Finland across Russia to Siberia and south to Afghanistan; it winters in India, Ceylon and Burma. There are no subspecies.

1959–1978 Two additional records

THICK-BILLED WARBLER—*Acrocephalus aedon*

PLATE 30

It resembles a Great Reed Warbler in size, shape and coloration; it is difficult to distinguish in the field, where the general coloration is olive brown above and paler below, with the more rufous rump providing a contrast. However, it has a *deeper and shorter bill with culmen distinctly down-curved*, wings shorter, tail longer in proportion and more graduated and rounded, and *lacks an eye-stripe*. In the hand identification is settled by the very long broad rounded first primary which in the Great Reed Warbler is a minute pin-like feather (see sketch). Legs blue. Length about 7¾ ins. (19·5 cms.).

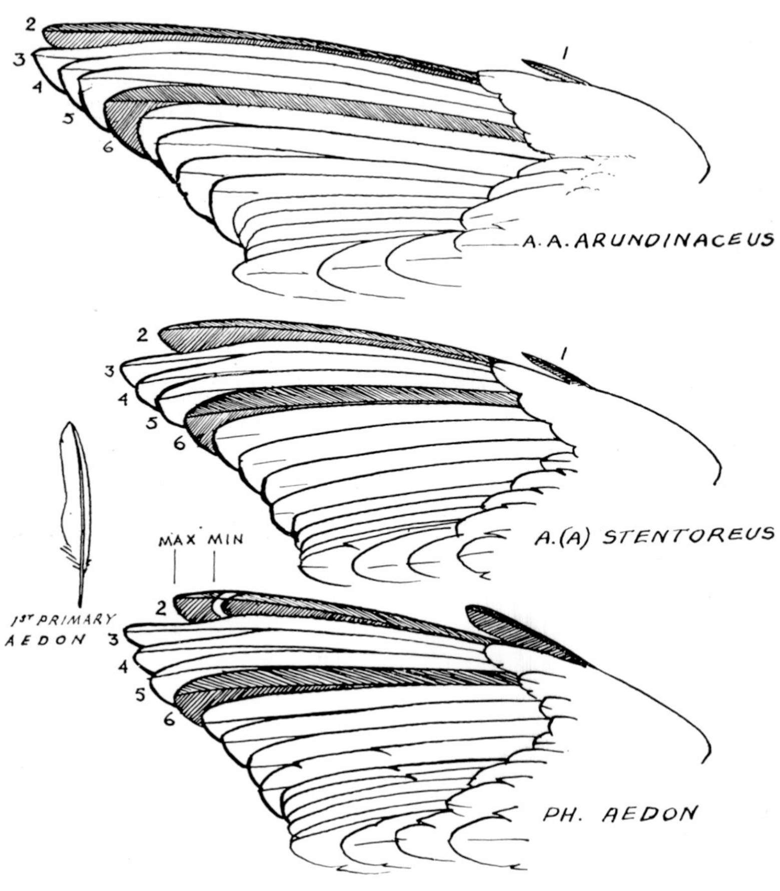

Habitat. In both summer and winter quarters it frequents bushes and scrub, particularly in damp places with long grass and along streams. The Fair Isle bird was found in a turnip-crop, before diving into dense reedy grass and *Heracleum*.

General Habits. It is a skulking bird, but when singing comes up to the top of bushes or trees.

Full song is loud and partly reminiscent of Icterine Warbler with loud, flute-like notes similar to those of the Nightingale, but a thin, low-pitched song may be heard on spring passage. The male's alarm call is a loud, harsh "chok-chok" or "tschak-tschak", sometimes more chattering.

Food appears to consist mainly of insects.

Status and Distribution. Scotland—One.

Trapped Fair Isle, Shetland, Oct. 6, 1955.

The bird breeds in S. Siberia, Mongolia, Manchuria, N.E. China and Korea; it winters in E. India, Burma, Indo-China and Andaman Islands. It is not known whether the British record refers to the eastern or the western race.

1959–1978 One additional record

OLIVACEOUS WARBLER—*Hippolais pallida*

PLATE 30

It has the wide bill and general appearance of this genus, but within the genus the head shape is important, the Melodious having an abrupt forehead and high rounded crown, that of Icterine being intermediate, while Olivaceous has a fairly flat forehead and crown. In spring and summer plumage the Olivaceous is distinguished from other European species of *Hippolais* (but only with difficulty from Booted Warbler) by *uniform greyish-olive upper-parts* (wings and tail darker) and *buffish-white under-parts* with a slightly darker suffusion on sides of breast; Icterine and Melodious Warblers are then lemon-yellow below. In autumn, however, young Melodious is pale yellow below, where Olivaceous has a buffish suffusion; Melodious retains a yellowish patch (lacking in Olivaceous) on the underwing at the carpal joint, and is darker brownish-olive on the upper-parts. The indistinct pale eye-stripe of Olivaceous as well as bill shape, should prevent confusion with the rather featureless Garden Warbler. Legs are bluish-grey. Length about 5 ins. (12·75 cms.).

Habitat. In the breeding season it haunts gardens, orchards, thickets and bushy places; often near water. In winter quarters it is chiefly found in groups of trees, gardens and savanna country.

General Habits. It is largely a tree-haunting species, but occurs more in small trees and scrub than in big timber. It is restless, but not shy, and fairly easily observed although keeping largely to cover.

Song is rather rambling and acrocephaline, and usually delivered from thick cover. The note is a sharp "tchack, tchack" or sparrow-like "chut". (Upcher's Warbler, *Hippolais languida*—a Middle Eastern bird of closely similar appearance but not on the British list, has a very distinctive note, passage migrants usually calling a loud "chuck" which is quite different from the sparrow-like chatter of Olivaceous or Melodious Warbler; and they constantly flick tail more like some chats than a warbler.)

Food is probably almost entirely small insects.

Status and Distribution. Great Britain—Two.

One seen and trapped Skokholm, Pembroke, Sept. 23–Oct. 3, 1951.

One trapped Portland, Dorset, Aug. 16, 1956.

The race concerned, *Hippolais pallida elaeica*, breeds in the Balkan peninsula and east to Afghanistan; other races occur in Spain, N. Africa, also in the Nile Valley. The bird winters in tropical Africa and S.W. Asia.

1959–1978 Ten additional records

BOOTED WARBLER—*Hippolais caligata*

PLATE 30

It is smaller than others of its genus. Greyish-brown above, inclining to rufous in autumn, and white below, washed buff or dull yellowish on sides and flanks, more strongly in young; the outermost tail-feathers are largely whitish. Eye-stripe is creamy. As a migrant to India it requires to be distinguished from Blyth's Reed-Warbler which is heavier and darker-looking, with larger bill, uniform-coloured and graduated, instead of almost square, tail and tends to be in trees, while Booted Warbler keeps chiefly to low cover. The Booted's rounded

Hippolais head separates it from Siberian Chiffchaff. In the hand, the wing measurements do not exceed 63 millimetres (according to the *Handbook*), while those of Olivaceous are minimum 63 mm. and Melodious minimum 63 mm.; these three species have very similar wing formulae. Legs pale or greyish-brown. Length about 4½ ins. (11·5 cms.).

Habitat. In breeding season it frequents bush-covered localities, low coppice growth and cane-brakes, on both marshy and dry ground; also cornfields, etc. In winter-quarters it is also found chiefly in low and thick scrub.

General Habits. It is extremely skulking; habits are otherwise without notable features.

It has the usual sharp "click" note common to many small warblers.

Food is mainly insects.

Status and Distribution. Scotland—One.

Female, Fair Isle, Shetland, Sept. 3, 1936.

The race concerned, *Hippolais caligata caligata*, breeds in Russia from near the Gulf of Finland east to the Yenisei valley in Siberia and south to Astrakhan. Other races occur south to Persia. It winters mainly in India.

1959–1978 Nine additional records

MELODIOUS WARBLER—*Hippolais polyglotta*

PLATE 30

It closely resembles Icterine Warbler. It is a stocky bird, slightly smaller than Garden Warbler, with a characteristic *contrast between yellow under-parts and brownish-olive upper-parts, and very high crown* giving it a "capped" look. In autumn some birds are more buffish than yellow on underparts. It is distinguishable from Icterine by its song, and (outside its winter quarters) lacks a pale patch on the closed wing. (This is a feature—more evident to some observers than others—possessed by the Icterine which apparently separates it from other British *Hippolais* as well as all *Sylvia* and *Phylloscopus* species; it is caused by pale fringes of the secondaries, tertials and greater coverts, and may vary from golden-yellow in spring to off-white in autumn, contrasting with the dark primaries.) It is also slightly smaller and more compact-looking than Icterine, with rounder head, and shorter, more rounded wings which give it a more fluttering flight; in the Icterine, on the other hand, the longer primaries give the closed wing a more tapering and pointed appearance, with a greater proportion of the length of the primaries extending beyond the rest of the wing. A pale yellow patch under the carpal joint of the wing of the Melodious is of value in the hand in helping separation from Olivaceous and Booted Warblers; the wing formula of the Olivaceous is similar to that of Melodious, while in the Booted Warbler it is a little different. Gape orange, as Icterine. Legs brownish (not so blue as Icterine). Length about 5 ins. (12·75 cms.).

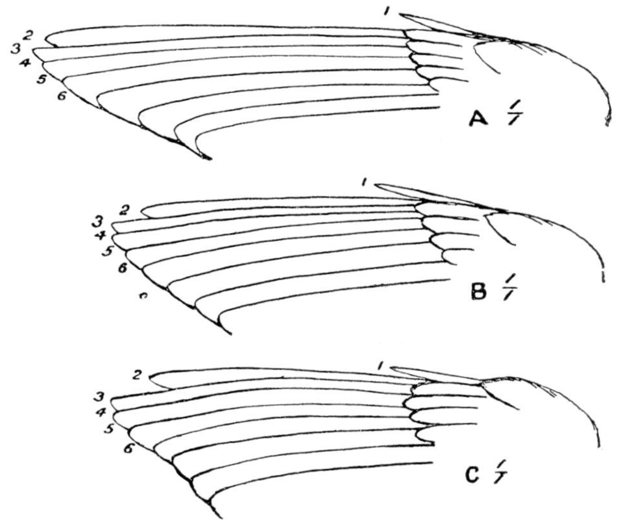

A. Icterine Warbler (*Hippolais icterina*). B. Melodious Warbler (*H. polyglotta*). C. Olivaceous Warbler (*H. pallida*). Note difference in lengths of 1st and 2nd primaries.

Habitat. It nests in fringes of trees and bushes along streams and roads, in gardens and open woodland, especially in damp places. It occurs more in gardens, etc., after the breeding season.

General Habits. Are much as Icterine Warbler; it keeps chiefly to higher bushes and trees. Active, restless and excitable, it is rather nervous of being watched in breeding season, but much less so in autumn and is seen more in open.

Typical note is a twitter or chatter much like Sparrow and quite different from the note of the Icterine Warbler. Autumn passage birds have a brief musical "hooeet", not unlike Icterine, Chiffchaff, etc. Song is markedly more subdued and less vehement than Icterine Warbler's, but is more musical and lacks the exaggerated harsh notes of that bird. It is very quick and hurried in delivery.

Food is chiefly insects. Some fruit is also taken.

Status and Distribution. Great Britain—A scarce but annual autumn visitor, to judge from the records since 1953 of birds trapped at the recently formed bird observatories. This new technique produced 16 or more records in 1958 alone, compared with a total of only 3 definite records in the *Handbook*. Most occur between mid-August and early October principally in S.W. England from Dorset westwards, and in the Irish Sea area at the islands of Skokholm (Pembroke), Bardsey (Caernarvon) and Great Saltee (Wexford), but there are a few records for May, June and July, and birds have reached east to Norfolk and north to Fair Isle (Shetland).

The species breeds in S.W. Europe from Portugal to Italy, and north to the Somme in France; also in N.W. Africa east to Tunisia. It winters in tropical West Africa. There are no subspecies.

1959–1978 Some hundreds of additional records

SUBALPINE WARBLER—*Sylvia cantillans*

PLATE 31

Pinkish to terracotta-coloured throat separated from grey upper-parts by a *white moustachial stripe* distinguish the male, though the brightness of colouring varies considerably and some are rather dull. The eye-ring is reddish in both sexes, at least in adults. A general effect of delicate grey, and white outer tail-feathers, aid recognition in flight. Female and young have the upper-parts drab brown and the throat buffish-white, more or less inclined to pink in old females. In the latter the moustachial stripe is usually recognizable in the field, but it may be barely perceptible in pale-throated birds, which look something like rather drab and buffish Lesser Whitethroats without dark ear-coverts, and are much paler (especially on crown) and *buffer* than female Sardinian Warbler. General form suggests a small, neckless, slightly-built Whitethroat. Bill is thin and pointed; legs flesh-pink. Length about $4\frac{3}{4}$ ins. (12 cms.).

Habitat. In breeding season it haunts thickets and bushy places usually in moister or more shady localities than Sardinian Warbler, often with scattered trees, including overgrown stream gullies, open woodland with rich undergrowth, thick hedgerows, bushy pastures, and so forth.

General Habits. It is usually very skulking, chiefly in low scrub, but also in the foliage of trees. Flight and movements are as Whitethroat.

Usual note is a sharp "tecc".

Food chiefly insects and their larvae.

Status and Distribution. British Isles—Sixteen, of which ten have occurred (nearly all trapped at bird observatories) during the last eight years (1951–1958). The records are widely scattered —Scillies, Pembroke, Wexford, Antrim, St. Kilda, Fair Isle (several), Ross, Isle of May, Norfolk. Five occurred in May (earliest 3rd), six in June, one July, three September and one October 1st.

The race concerned, *Sylvia cantillans cantillans*, breeds in S. Europe from Portugal to Italy. Other races occur in N.W. Africa and east Mediterranean countries of Europe and Asia. A partial migrant, some birds reaching Sudan in winter.

1959–1978 58 additional records

SARDINIAN WARBLER—*Sylvia melanocephala*

PLATE 31

The male has a *glossy black cap extending below eye*, a pure *white throat*, slate-grey mantle and blackish graduated tail with white at the sides, conspicuous in flight. The first two characters alone distinguish it from all other warblers except the much larger Orphean, which has the cap browner and less well-defined, mantle a browner grey, and a nearly square tail. The browner female is less distinctive, being a rather dark-looking warbler, with cap only slightly darker and greyer than the back; otherwise it is not unlike Lesser Whitethroat, but darker and warmer brown above, while the graduated tail, constantly spread, is a useful character. Eye-ring is brick-red in adult male, paler in female. There is sometimes a slight pink tinge on the breast; this is more strongly marked in eastern races and may cause confusion with Subalpine Warbler. Young in autumn resemble adults, but male is duller. Build and outline of head (steep forehead) are much like a small Whitethroat. Length about 5¼ ins. (13–13·5 cms.).

Habitat. In breeding season it frequents thickets and bushy places with or without trees, often arid; gardens are more frequented in winter.

General Habits. Though restless and inquisitive it is often exceedingly skulking, especially in autumn, when the highly characteristic scolding-note often proclaims the presence and identity of an unseen bird. Flight, carriage, etc., are as Whitethroat.

Usual notes (very distinctive) are an extremely hard, harsh stuttering "stitititititicc" and, somewhat less frequently, "treek-treek-treek", of the same character.

Food is chiefly small insects, also spiders; in autumn and winter also eats figs and other fruit and seeds.

Status and Distribution. England—One.

Adult male trapped Lundy, Devon, May 10, 1955.

The species breeds in the Mediterranean countries of Europe, the Canary Islands, N. Africa and in Asia east to Afghanistan. The race to which the British record belonged was not determined.

1959–1978 Five additional records

ORPHEAN WARBLER—*Sylvia hortensis*

PLATE 31

It can only be confused with male Blackcap and Sardinian Warbler, and the resemblance to these is only rather superficial. Larger than the Blackcap, it is greyer above, with *dark cap extending below the eye and not sharply defined behind, and has a white throat and white in outer tail feathers.* It is much larger than Sardinian; its cap is dull brownish instead of glossy jet-black, and shades off into the grey of mantle instead of being clearly demarcated, while the tail is almost square instead of graduated. The crown is not so dark in female and hardly darker than the mantle in young birds. The latter in autumn can look like large Lesser Whitethroat or might be confused with young Barred Warblers which, however, have longer tails and upper tail-coverts with light tips. The shape of the head is Whitethroat-like, rather than Blackcap-like, the raising of the crown-feathers tending to give a peaked appearance, as in the former species. Usually pale yellowish-white eye is a good field character. Legs are dark grey. Length about 6 ins. (15 cms.).

Habitat. It breeds in open cork, ilex and other woods with undergrowth, also orchards and gardens. In winter-quarters it appears to frequent largely riverside scrub.

General Habits. Though also seen in low bushes, it spends much of its time in the foliage of trees.

Scolding note is a hard, rattling "trrrrr" recalling Sardinian Warbler's, but without its extreme hardness and metallic quality, and is less prolonged; also a Blackcap-like "tac, tac". Song is a rich and pleasant warble of thrush-like quality without harsh or strident notes, of which the chief feature is a regularly repetitive character; when heard for the first time one is inclined to look for a thrush rather than a warbler.

Food is chiefly insects and their larvae. Fruit and berries are also eaten in autumn and winter.

Status and Distribution. England—Two.

Female shot near Wetherby, Yorks., July 6, 1848.

One trapped Portland, Dorset, Sept. 20, 1955.

The race concerned, *Sylvia hortensis hortensis*, breeds in N.W. Africa and in Europe from Iberian peninsula east to N. Italy and north to Luxemburg; it winters in Sahara and tropical Africa. Another race occurs from Balkan peninsula east to Turkestan.

1959–1978 One additional record

GREENISH WARBLER—*Phylloscopus trochiloides*

PLATE 32

About the size and shape of a Chiffchaff, but with a *single whitish or yellowish wing-bar*, and a prominent long yellowish-white stripe above the eye, almost straight and reaching nearly to the nape; under-parts yellowish-white or whitish. The wing-bar is sometimes fairly prominent, but is sometimes rendered very inconspicuous or even invisible by abrasion. The degree of wear is not always uniform, and the wing-bar may be discernible on one of a bird's wings after it has disappeared from the other wing. In worn plumage the bird can look greyish, rather than greenish, especially on head, nape and rump. On passage it is difficult to separate from the larger Arctic Warbler, unless latter is in fresh plumage showing the double wing-bar, but the *darker, purplish-brown leg* colour and the short weak bill of the Greenish may prove helpful. In the hand the shorter second and longer first primaries distinguish it (compare sketch under Arctic Warbler); moreover the primaries are emarginated on feathers nos. 3–6 (Arctic on 3–5), and tail feathers are edged whitish on inner web (unlike Chiffchaff). Bill horn, lower mandible orange at base. Length about 4¼ ins. (11 cms.).

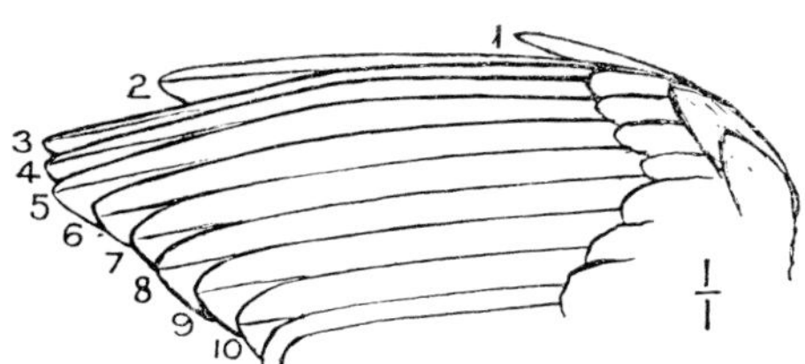

The Greenish Warbler (*Phylloscopus trochiloides*). Note shorter 2nd and longer 1st primaries than in Arctic Warbler.

Habitat. In the breeding season it is found chiefly on wood edge or in open woodland, deciduous or coniferous, but especially spruce with scattered deciduous. In winter quarters in varied situations with trees.

General Habits. It keeps for the most part fairly high up in the foliage of trees, restless in the breeding season but in winter quarters a quiet bird creeping about in foliage. One searching for food on Fair Isle very often carried the wing-tips below the level of the back, and flicked wings and tail spasmodically like Hedge Sparrow.

The usual call, often in tree-tops, is a musical double note "chee-wee", the first note not unlike that of Chiffchaff, the second lower and flatter. Song, usually from canopy, is short, hurried and powerful; it is usually introduced by a few notes like the call, followed by a Wren-like trill and a short, rapid medley of notes of varying pitch, but there is much variation in detail. Song may occur on spring or autumn passage.

Food consists chiefly of insects.

Status and Distribution. British Isles—Although only one record was included in the *Handbook*, there have been over a dozen more from 1945 to 1958, and probably both the bird's extension of range westwards in the Baltic area and the establishment of bird observatories at strategic places on the British coasts have contributed to this increase. Most have occurred on the east side, from Fair Isle to Dungeness, but there are also records from Great Saltee (Wexford) and Bardsey Island (Caernarvon); mainly in September, but one or two June, July and August, and one November 23.

The race concerned, *Phylloscopus trochiloides viridanus*, breeds right across north-central Europe and Asia from the Baltic to Mongolia and south to Kashmir; it has recently bred in Sweden. Other races occur in Caucasia, Persia, Himalayas, China and across E. Siberia. The bird winters from India to Indo-China.

1959–1978 116 additional records

ARCTIC WARBLER—*Phylloscopus borealis*

PLATE 32

It appears a distinctly larger, and also slimmer bird than Willow Warbler, with upper-parts greenish grey-brown, *under-parts whitish and creamy wing-bar* usually tolerably noticeable at close range although it may occasionally be lost in worn plumage of adults in autumn. The second (upper) wing-bar, faint and yellower, is seldom visible at all in the field, and then only in fresh plumage—e.g. young birds in autumn. Adults are a brighter, greyer green than young birds, whose upper-parts are a dark greenish-olive. The long broad light yellowish eye-stripe is very prominent, being bounded by a more definite dark mark below than in the common species. *Legs are a rather pale brownish-flesh* (those of Greenish are dark), and the orange-brown bill is long and dagger-like. See also Greenish Warbler. In the hand the two species may be separated by the differences in wing formula shown in the sketches. Length about $4\frac{3}{4}$ ins. (12 cms.).

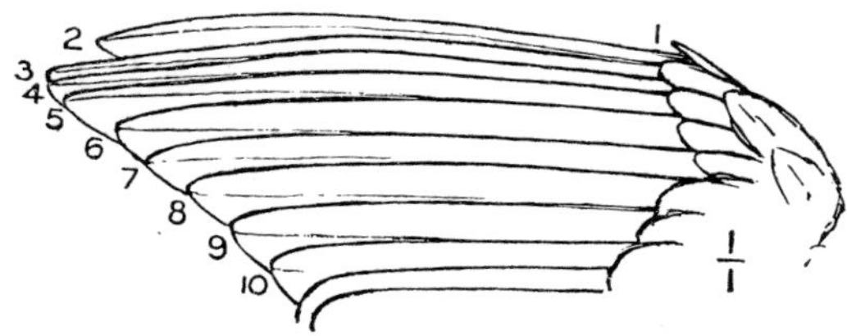

Arctic Warbler (*Phylloscopus borealis*). Note longer 2nd and shorter 1st primaries than in Greenish Warbler.

Habitat. In the breeding season it frequents well-grown birch and conifer woods with good undergrowth. It likes the neighbourhood of water. In winter quarters in Malaya it has been found mostly near coast, among mangroves, etc., and not in heavy jungle, though ascending to 3,500 ft.

General Habits. It behaves much like other leaf warblers, hopping and flitting about amongst foliage and sometimes hovering in the air for a moment to peck an insect from a leaf. It keeps largely to the canopy, but also occurs sometimes in lower vegetation.

The chief note on the breeding grounds is a metallic clicking "tzick", often preceding the Cirl Bunting-like song; also a low rattle, like Mistle Thrush's scold very much softened down, and a rather hoarse little "tswee-ip". Migrants also give a hard, emphatic "zik".

Food consists of insects.

Status and Distribution. Great Britain—About twenty, mainly on Fair Isle, Shetland, but also recorded from several east coast localities south to Blakeney, Norfolk. Most have occurred in late August or September, latest date October 24.

The race concerned, *Phylloscopus borealis borealis*, breeds across N. Europe and Siberia from N. Scandinavia to the Bering Sea, and winters in S.E. Asia. Other races occur in Japan, Kamchatka and Alaska.

1959–1978 79 additional records

PALLAS'S WARBLER—*Phylloscopus proregulus*

PLATE 32

The *primrose-yellow rump* is at once very obvious except when the wings are closed, but one usually sees it hovering with rapidly whirling wings searching for insects among outer foliage. This habit and its very small size make it look like a Goldcrest, and it has a pale double wing-bar. When amongst thick foliage it is very difficult to find, and must generally first be located by its note. Not only the rump, but bright green upper-parts, *broad pale yellow stripe down the centre of the crown* and yellower eye-stripe separate it from Yellow-browed Warbler. Length about 3½ ins. (9 cms.).

Habitat. It nests in birch, conifer, and mixed forest. In winter-quarters it is found mainly in tree tops.

General Habits. Behaviour and flight are actually more Goldcrest-like than phylloscopine, but the Northumberland bird was more prone to hover, apt to flit further between bouts of searching, and seldom hung upside down.

Note is a small, soft, but quite phylloscopine "weesp", shriller and more prolonged than that of Yellow-browed Warbler, and described as consisting of two distinct notes, the second higher than first and not slurred into one another as in Yellow-browed.

Food consists of insects chiefly taken from trees or on the wing.

Status and Distribution. England—Four.

Female Cley, Norfolk, Oct. 31, 1896.

One seen and trapped Seahouses, Northumberland, Oct. 13–14, 1951.

One trapped near Holme, Norfolk, Nov. 17, 1957.

One seen Sandwich, Kent, Nov. 23, 1958.

The race concerned, *Phylloscopus proregulus proregulus*, breeds in S. Siberia from Krasnovarsk east to Sakhalin; it winters in S.E. Asia. Other races occur in the Himalayas and China.

1959–1978 110 additional records

RADDE'S WARBLER—*Phylloscopus schwarzi*

PLATE 33

Resembles the Dusky Warbler, but upper-parts are not so dark and usually more olive, less rufous; it has a considerably stouter bill and stouter, more yellowish legs; prominent superciliary stripe. Length about 5 ins. (12·75 cms.).

Habitat. In the breeding-season it haunts deciduous woods and bushy borders of woodland, especially where there are small streams. In winter-quarters, thick scrub and bush cover.

General Habits. Usually keeps well concealed in bushes and high grasses. It perches in an upright attitude like an *Acrocephalus* and not like a *Phylloscopus*.

Notes are variously described as "gibout-gibout", a nervous soft "twit-twit" and as "disproportionately loud".

Food is probably insects.

Status and Distribution. England—One.

North Cotes, Lincs., Oct. 1, 1898.

The species breeds in south-central and E. Siberia east to Korea and Sakhalin; it winters from S. China and S. Burma to Siam. There are no subspecies.

1959–1978 24 additional records

DUSKY WARBLER—*Phylloscopus fuscatus*

PLATE 33

It is the only leaf warbler on British list with *no trace of green or yellow in adult plumage*, and has been compared in coloration to a warm-coloured Reed Warbler with a very prominent pale buff eye-stripe. Upper-parts are fairly warm grey-brown, darkest on head, wings and tail; sides warm buff, rest of under-parts paler. It resembles Radde's Warbler but the latter has, according to descriptions, quite a different and very loud note. Legs brown. Length about 4¼ ins. (11 cms.).

Habitat. In the breeding season it haunts deciduous woods on sides of lower hills, especially those bordering swamps but also on arid mountains. In winter-quarters frequents scrub, low bushes, reeds, paddy, and heavy grass.

General Habits. Although it has been compared to a Reed Warbler, it has the typical horizontal carriage, flattish head and wing-fluttering action of a leaf warbler, but is much more of a ground feeder; habits are skulking.

The usual note is a single "tek".

Food is mainly small insects.

Status and Distribution. Scotland—One.

Female, Auskerry, Orkney, Oct. 1, 1913.

The race concerned, *Phylloscopus fuscatus fuscatus*, breeds from Tomsk east to Anadyr and Sakhalin and south to Inner Mongolia; another race occurs in E. Tibet and central China. It winters from N.E. India and S. China to Siam.

1959–1978 24 additional records

BONELLI'S WARBLER—*Phylloscopus bonelli*

PLATE 30

A leaf warbler with *greyish-white under-parts, and rump yellowish* in contrast to the earth-brown or grey-brown (colour of Garden Warbler) of the rest of the upper-parts; it has a pale super-ciliary stripe. There is a touch of bright yellow at the bend of the closed wing and a yellowish green patch on the wing is made by the edges of primaries. The colour of the rump, which is generally covered by the wing and difficult to see in the field, is the best distinction from the Chiffchaff, while the Willow Warbler additionally differs in having some yellow on the underparts. Legs brown, sometimes pale, sometimes darker than is normal for Willow Warbler. Length about 4½ ins. (11·5 cms.).

Habitat. In breeding season it frequents chiefly open mixed woodland often with plenty of conifers, nesting for the most part on dry hillsides, up to 6,000 ft. preferring a southerly aspect at least in the northern part of its range.

General Habits. It is largely a bird of the upper foliage, active and agile, making frequent little sallies when feeding; but it remains unobtrusive.

The call "hu-eet" resembles that of Willow Warbler but is less plaintive. The song is a monotone, a dry trill of about half-a-dozen notes rattled off just too fast to count the exact number; it is rather like the opening part of the corresponding song of Wood Warbler, and at a distance confusion with Cirl Bunting is possible.

Food is mainly if not entirely insects.

Status and Distribution. Great Britain—Four.

Female trapped and later killed Skokholm, Pembroke, Aug. 31, 1948.

One trapped Lundy, Devon, Sept. 1, 1954.

One trapped Portland, Dorset, Aug. 29, 1955.

One seen Marazion Marsh, Cornwall, Sept. 14, 1958.

The race probably concerned, *Phylloscopus bonelli bonelli*, breeds from Portugal to Italy and north to Belgium and Czechoslovakia, also in N. Africa from Morocco to Tunisia; it winters in tropical W. Africa. Another race occurs in the Balkan peninsula, Asia Minor and Palestine.

1959–1978 56 additional records

COLLARED FLYCATCHER—*Ficedula albicollis*

PLATE 33

The male in summer is distinguished from Pied Flycatcher by *white collar* and greyish-white rump; it has also more white at the base of the primaries and on forehead and less at the sides of tail. The females of these two species are more difficult to separate, but female Collared has *upper-parts greyer and some have a collar indicated by a pale shadow*; it also usually has a more pronounced white wing-bar. In autumn the blacks of the males are replaced by brown; the birds have considerably less white on the collar and wings, so that they may resemble female, but some retain whitish on rump; they are said to show a distinct light moustachial stripe extending below the ear-coverts to form a half-collar. Length is about 5 ins. (12·75 cms.).

Habitat. It is found in much the same types of locality as Pied Flycatcher: woods and groves, especially oak and beech, well timbered parks, avenues, orchards, etc.; commonly near water.

General Habits. Its habits are like Pied Flycatcher, but it feeds more in trees and less on the ground and, like that species, is said to be difficult to observe after the young are fledged.

Song is described as resembling Pied Flycatcher's but latter is louder and more distinctly divided. Call notes are a loud "hwee" and "zig zig".

Food is probably almost entirely insects.

Status and Distribution. Great Britain—Two.

Adult male shot Whalsay, Shetland, May 11, 1947.

Male seen Bardsey, Caernarvon, May 10, 1957.

The species breeds from E. France north to Baltic and east to S.E. Europe and S. Russia; it winters in central and N. Africa and S.W. Asia. There are no subspecies.

1959–1978 Six additional records

ISABELLINE SHRIKE—*Lanius isabellinus*

PLATE 34

The Isabelline Shrike is an obvious shrike from shape and carriage, and is closely related to Red-backed Shrike. The male in winter plumage (as it was seen on the Isle of May) is a strikingly pale bird. The *upper-parts are pale greyish buff*, warmer on the nape and crown. The *rump and tail are clear rufous.* A black band from bill to ear-coverts runs through the eye, and above it is a whitish stripe. The cheeks and under-parts are often conspicuously white, but with a varying amount of pinkish buff on the flanks. A white patch at the base of the primaries forms a prominent bar when wing is spread. In summer all the upper-parts of male are darker, and the female resembles the winter male but is even paler and may show crescentic marks on under-parts. Young birds are duller and have crescentic markings on breast and wing-coverts. Bill and legs blackish. Length about 6¾ ins. (17 cms.).

Habitat. It is a bird of thorny desert scrub, steppe bushes and thinly wooded areas.

General Habits. In habits and food it resembles Red-backed Shrike.

Status and Distribution. Scotland.

One seen Isle of May, Fife, Sept. 26, 1950.

The bird breeds across central Asia from Transcaspia to Mongolia; it winters in tropical Africa. It is not known to which race the British record refers.

1959–1978 12 additional records. *Lanius isabellinus* is now again regarded as a full species

RED-EYED VIREO—*Vireo olivaceus*

PLATE 34

The vireos are an American family of rather warbler-like birds not unlike leaf warblers in general coloration, but with more solid proportions, heavier bill and deliberate movements. The Red-eyed Vireo is the commonest species and the only one which has occurred in the British Isles. It is characterized by a *grey crown above a long clear white eye-stripe which is narrowly bordered with black on both sides*. Otherwise the upper-parts are rather uniform olive green, and under-parts whitish, greyer on the flanks. The sexes are similar. Bill is blackish and legs pale lead-grey. The eye is red in adults. Length about 6¼ ins. (16 cms.). The Black-whiskered Vireo (*Vireo altiloquus*) is very similar apart from a narrow black streak on each side of the throat; the Warbling Vireo (*Vireo gilvus*) has the crown the same colour as mantle and a slight eye-stripe lacking the black borders; other N. American vireos have yellow on flanks or breast, and most of them also have a double white wing-bar.

Habitat. A bird of deciduous woodland, copses, orchards and shade trees, frequenting chiefly the upper branches, although nesting low.

General Habits. It moves slowly but almost continuously about the twigs, without the nervous actions and flutterings of a warbler. A confiding bird.

Song is very persistent but monotonous, consisting of a series of short abrupt phrases of three or four notes, with a very small range of pitch. A common note is "chway".

Food is chiefly insects taken from the foliage. It also eats berries in autumn, and seeds.

Status and Distribution. Ireland—One.

Picked up dead Tuskar Rock Lighthouse, Wexford, Oct. 4, 1951.

The species breeds in N. America across central Canada and south to Colorado, Texas and Florida; it winters in S. America. There are no subspecies.

1959–1978 Nine additional records

CITRIL FINCH—*Serinus citrinella*

PLATE 35

Linnet-like form and *predominantly yellowish-green plumage shading into grey on the nape and sides of neck* distinguish adults. The *rump is greenish-yellow*, the under-parts unstreaked. Wings and tail are blackish, with a yellow-green wing-bar. Colours are brightest in the male; the female is more streaked and duller. Young birds are rather nondescript, lacking any green or yellow; they are predominantly greyish-brown with paler under-parts, streaked dark above and below, and with darker wings and tail. They soon begin to show some greenish, however. Length about 4¾ ins. (12 cms.).

Habitat. It is normally confined to mountains, affecting principally broken ground on the outskirts of conifer forest but, in autumn especially, is often found far from any trees. In winter it descends to lower levels amongst mountains, but rarely to plains.

General Habits. Flight and behaviour recall Goldfinch. It perches on trees, but also settles freely on rocks, etc., and spends much time on the ground. Sociable.

The flight-note is a rather nasal and "creaky", distinctively metallic "tweck", commonly becoming a twittering "tweck-eck-eck-eck". Call is a plaintive, rather musical, piping "tsuu". The song, uttered in short phrases, is somewhat Siskin-like.

Food consists chiefly of seeds of fir and spruce, as well as of various ground-plants, also buds, berries and small insects.

Status and Distribution. England—One.

Female caught by a bird-catcher on Yarmouth Denes, on the flat E. Norfolk coast on January 29, 1904.

Abroad the race concerned, *Serinus citrinella citrinella*, is found in the mountain system of southern and central Europe north to the Alps and S. Germany. Another race occurs in Corsica and Sardinia.

1959–1978 No additional records

PARROT CROSSBILL—*Loxia pytyopsittacus*

Taxonomic opinions have changed a number of times regarding the relationships of the crossbills occurring in Britain. Currently (1979), Parrot Crossbill, common Crossbill *Loxia curvirostra* and Scottish Crossbill *Loxia scotica* are regarded as three separate species. All three are identical in plumage, and readers are referred to the account of the Crossbill in the *Popular Handbook of British Birds*. While the Parrot Crossbill is slightly larger than the Crossbill, its bill is disproportionately heavier, strikingly stout and arched on both mandibles, and giving a distinctive appearance, as shown in the accompanying sketch. The Scottish Crossbill is intermediate in size, and its

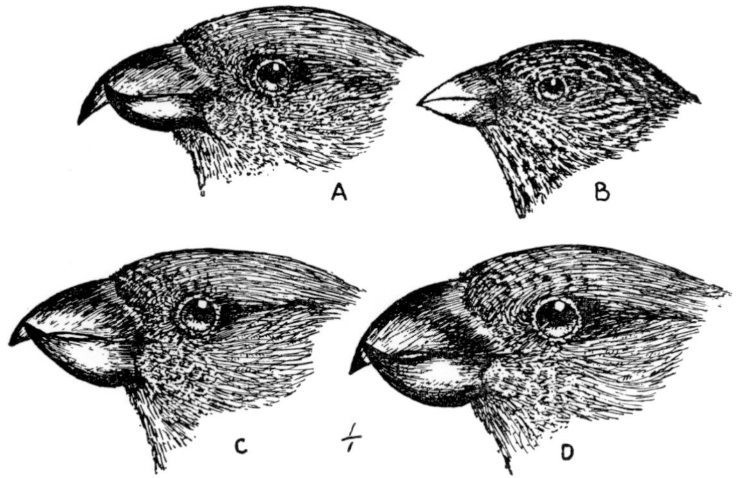

Crossbill (*Loxia curvirostra*). A. Adult. B. Nestling.
C. Scottish Crossbill (*Loxia scotica*). D. Parrot Crossbill (*Loxia pytyopsittacus*).

bill is only slightly less heavy than Parrot Crossbill's; satisfactory separation in the field would be unlikely but fortunately the Scottish Crossbill is thought to be strictly resident, breeding in the Scottish highlands. Elsewhere most Parrot Crossbills should be identifiable on a good view.

Habits also are similar, but in N. Europe the Parrot Crossbill tends to prefer pines and Crossbill to prefer spruce. The voice of Parrot Crossbill is deeper.

Status and Distribution. Great Britain—About ten, 1818–1954, most in S.E. England.

The species breeds in Scandinavia, Finland and N. Russia, sporadically south to Poland, and often moves farther south into central Europe in winter.

1959–1978 About 80 additional records during winter 1962–63, and one in 1975

BLACK-AND-WHITE WARBLER—*Mniotilta varia*

PLATE 34

A distinctive bird with *striped black and white plumage above and below*, especially on the head, and a double white wing-bar. The female is similar but is less definitely marked, has less streaking below, lacks the male's black throat and has a brownish wash on flanks. In young birds the pattern is the same but is less sharply contrasted, the black being more brownish and the white suffused with buff. Confusion is unlikely with any other species on the British list, or indeed with other American warblers except the spring male Blackpoll Warbler (*Dendroica striata*) which has the crown completely black down to eye level, and white cheeks below, whereas the Black-and-White Warbler has striped crown, and mainly blackish cheeks. Bill black; legs dark brown. Length about 5¼ ins. (13–13·5 cms.).

Habitat. It is found in all types of woodland, commonly in deciduous and mixed, more locally in coniferous woods; it also visits orchards and parkland but rarely occurs away from trees.

General Habits. It has a highly characteristic habit of working like a woodpecker or tree-creeper up, down or spirally on upright trunks and main branches of trees, searching the bark for insects, but without using tail for support. It also feeds in foliage, moving slowly but tirelessly, and occasionally takes an insect in the air. Does not form flocks but outside the breeding season often joins wandering bands of nuthatches, creepers, tits.

Call notes are a weak "tsip" and a louder "chink".

Food consists of insects.

Status and Distribution. Scotland—One.

Found dead Scalloway, Shetland, mid-October, 1936.

The species breeds in eastern N. America from Mackenzie to Newfoundland and south to Texas; it winters from southern U.S.A. to S. America. There are no subspecies.

1959–1978 Three additional records

YELLOW-RUMPED WARBLER (or MYRTLE WARBLER)—*Dendroica coronata*

PLATE 35

The numerous warblers of North America belong to the family of wood warblers, the Parulidae, which is not represented in Europe, although a few examples have occurred here as vagrants. Many other species might conceivably be recorded in the future, and as they would probably be in their confusing autumn plumages, the observer fortunate enough to see one should take a detailed description, noting especially the presence or absence of wing-bars and tail-markings, the distribution of streaks on the upper and under parts, and the colour of the legs and undertail coverts.

The Yellow-rumped Warbler is one of the best known American warblers. Adults are distinguished at all seasons by *lemon-yellow patches on the rump, on the sides of the breast* and (at times hard to see) on the crown. The male in summer has bluish-grey upper-parts streaked with black, and whitish under-parts, heavily marked with black on the breast and sides; black cheeks and ear-coverts; whitish eye-stripe and double wing-bar; a noticeable amount of white in outer tail feathers. In winter the black on side of head is lost, the upper-parts become brown and the under-parts less heavily marked. The female is duller, with cheeks, wings and tail brown where the male is black, the whites less clean, and the four yellow patches are more subdued; winter plumage is substantially the same. The immature has dull eye-stripe, wing-bars and tail pattern; it has the conspicuous yellow rump-patch, and concealed crown-spot, but sometimes lacks the yellow patches on the sides of the body. When the bird is on the ground (in winter) it has something of the appearance of a Meadow Pipit. Bill and legs are black. Length about 5½ ins. (14 cms.).

Habitat. Although restricted to conifers, and especially spruce forests, for nesting, at other seasons it occurs almost anywhere where there are trees and bushes.

General Habits. It is a hardy species of warbler, less dependent than most on insects; it can subsist for long periods on berries and seeds for which it searches not only in branches but also on the ground where it will even take bread-crumbs. Thus it regularly survives periods of frost and snow. In winter it often occurs in loose flocks in open bushy areas, and is not at all shy. The Devon bird was noticeably pugnacious, chasing tits and finches from the neighbourhood of the bird-table which was its headquarters.

The call is a loud "check".

Food is largely insects in summer and berries in winter; sometimes seeds. Household scraps are also taken, the Devon bird being particularly partial to marmalade.

Status and Distribution. England—One.

Seen and finally found dead Newton St. Cyres, Devon, Jan. 4–Feb. 10, 1955.

The species breeds from Alaska to Newfoundland and south to the northern U.S.A.; it winters on W. coast of U.S.A., and in east from about New York, south to Panama.

1959–1978 Six additional records

NORTHERN WATERTHRUSH—*Seiurus noveboracensis*

PLATE 36

This American warbler resembles a small wagtail or pipit more than a thrush. The upper-parts are uniform dark brown; the long broad *eye-stripe is pale yellowish buff and very prominent; under-parts are pale yellow*, with throat, breast and flanks heavily striped with black. There is no white in the tail. The sexes are similar, and the summer and winter plumages are alike. The brown bill is wagtail-like, legs are flesh coloured. Length about 6 ins. (15 cms.).

The Louisiana Waterthrush (*Seiurus motacilla*), which has not been recorded this side of the Atlantic, is separated by its white eye-stripe, white under-parts (buffer on flanks), and throat unspotted and unmarked apart from a moustachial stripe at the sides. Some Northerns, however, have almost white eye-stripes and under-parts. The Ovenbird (*S. aurocapillus*) looks somewhat similar, but is a woodland bird, with a greener back and an orange crown-stripe.

Habitat. It breeds in shady swamps, but at other seasons is less restricted to the vicinity of water, and on passage may be found in gardens under the shade of shrubs. The bird which occurred in the Scillies spent several days along the sea shore.

General Habits. Most of its time is spent on the ground or in low bushes but it will at times perch higher. It feeds mainly along banks of streams and ponds, much like a Common Sandpiper, with the same constant bobbing of head and tail, walking on stones and logs in the water and even wading.

Song is loud and ends with a diagnostic "chew-chew-chew" dropping in pitch. Call is "spik", sharp and explosive, with some tonal resemblance to that of Grey Wagtail.

Food is largely insects, also small molluscs, crustaceans, worms and fish.

Status and Distribution. England—One.

Seen and trapped St. Agnes, Scilly Isles, Sept. 30–Oct. 12, 1958.

The species breeds from Alaska across Canada to Newfoundland and in northern U.S.A.; it winters from Florida to northern S. America. Several races have been described.

1959–1978 One additional record

YELLOWTHROAT—*Geothlypis trichas*

PLATE 36

The adult male is readily recognized by the *broad black mask which covers the forehead and extends backwards, embracing the eye, and down on to the cheeks*. Behind the black is (usually) a grey band over the top of the crown, the ear-coverts, and on to sides of neck; otherwise the upper-parts are olive-brown, greener on back of head and rump. The under-parts are lemon-yellow, brightest on the throat, and shading to brownish on the flanks. This plumage is retained by the adult in winter; but the immature male has no more than traces of the mask indicated to a varying extent by dark grey, often mottled, and the top of the head is mainly olive. The female lacks distinctive features, being browner above and buffer below than male, but with rich yellow throat and white belly, and having head mainly olive-brown without black or grey markings. Neither sex has wing-bar or eye-stripe. In autumn the female and young may be distinguished from similar American warblers by the *white belly*. The legs of the Lundy bird were pale pinkish-brown, and bill horn-coloured. Length about 5 ins. (12·75 cms.).

Habitat. It is typically associated with water, frequenting low vegetation in marshes and on the borders of streams and damp thickets, but it is also found at times in shrubberies and clearings in dry situations.

General Habits. While in general it resembles a small, round-winged leaf-warbler, some movements are very wren-like. It dodges quickly into and out of cover, and when disturbed flies only a short distance before seeking cover again. Frequently cocks up its tail.

The usual call is a harsh and loud "tchep"; the song a rapid phrase of 3 or 4 clear notes repeated several times: "witchity, witchity, witchity, witch".

Food is mainly insects.

Status and Distribution. England—One.

Immature male trapped Lundy, Devon, Nov. 4, 1954.

The species breeds from Alaska across Canada to Newfoundland and south to Mexico; it winters from southern U.S.A. to West Indies and Central America. It is not known to which race the British record refers.

1959–1978 No additional records

SUMMER TANAGER—*Piranga rubra*

PLATE 37

The adult male is a *uniform scarlet-rose all over* and at all seasons. The female is greenish above and golden-yellow below, lacking wing-bars or other distinctive pattern, and the wings are greenish, not much darker than mantle. Young males in autumn resemble females but are more orange coloured. The substantial bill is sparrow-like but longer, and whitish in colour; legs horn. Length about $7\frac{1}{2}$ ins. (19 cms.).

Female and immatures have to be distinguished from Scarlet Tanager, which see for differences.

Habitat. It frequents dry, open woodland, deciduous or mixed, with trees small or mature.

General Habits. A rather retiring and solitary bird with very deliberate movements, for the most part keeping to the foliage of trees, but it will hawk insects on the wing.

Note is a staccato "pit-ush-tuck". (Scarlet Tanager has a distinctive "chip-buzz".)

Food is mainly insects, particularly bees and wasps, also spiders; fruit and berries are also taken.

Status and Distribution. Wales—One.

Immature male seen and trapped Bardsey Island, Caernarvon, Sept. 11–25, 1957.

The species breeds from east-central U.S.A. south to Florida and Mexico; it winters from Mexico south to Peru.

1959–1978 No additional records

WHITE-THROATED SPARROW—*Zonotrichia albicollis*

PLATE 37

The American sparrows are a numerous group of species related to the buntings, and belonging to an entirely different family from the European sparrows. The White-throated Sparrow is brown above, the mantle feathers having darker centres, and the cheeks and under-parts are grey like a Dunnock. The distinctive features are on the head: the *clear-cut white throat, white-centred black crown,* a broad conspicuous *eye-stripe which is yellow between eye and bill but white behind the eye* where it is separated from the cheek by a narrow black stripe running from eye to nape. A double whitish wing-bar is not very sharply defined. The sexes are similar. Immatures have the crown brownish with a paler centre and the broad eye-stripe is tawny buff throughout its length; under-parts are dull grey-brown, with indistinct dark streaks on breast and flanks, a slight moustachial stripe on the side of the throat, and a white throat. The bunting-like bill is horn, legs pale brown. Length about 6¾ ins. (17 cms.).

The head-markings alone should distinguish it from any of the duller European buntings. The large size and lack of heavy breast streakings distinguish it from other American sparrows except White-crowned (*Z. leucophrys*) which lacks the white throat and has unmarked greyish cheeks and breast and a pink bill at all ages. The Swamp Sparrow (*Melospiza georgiana*) also has a white throat, but is much smaller and warmer brown on crown and back. The Song Sparrow (*M. melodia*) has heavily streaked under-parts, the streaks coalescing to form a large dark spot in the centre of the breast.

Habitat. Dunnock-like, it haunts thickets, small trees, brushwood and all kinds of bushy places, whether in suburban gardens or forest clearings. It will also visit cornfields and places with tall weeds.

General Habits. Usually keeps on or near the ground where it searches for food, scratching among the dead leaves. When flushed it seldom flies far or perches high, preferring to hide in low cover. At times collects into parties. Call is a metallic "chink", or a slurred "tseet". The song is a clear, sweet whistle likened to "Oh, Sweet Canada, Canada, Canada".

Food is seeds, berries and insects.

Status and Distribution. Scotland—One.

Male shot Flannan Islands, May 18, 1909.

The species breeds in N. America from Yukon to Newfoundland and south to northern U.S.A.; it winters almost entirely in U.S.A. There are no subspecies.

1959–1978 11 additional records

PINE BUNTING—*Emberiza leucocephalos*

PLATE 38

The chestnut throat and broad band through the eye, and black-bordered white crown and cheeks are distinctive of the male. The under-parts are dull white, with an ill-defined brownish breast-band. The rest is much as in Yellowhammer, including rufous rump and white in tail. The head pattern is obscured in autumn. Female is much like female Yellowhammer, with white replacing yellow. Young birds differ from other British buntings with white abdomens, in having the combination of chestnut rump and brown lesser wing-coverts, whereas Rustic Bunting has both chestnut, Little Bunting both brown, and Reed Bunting has lesser coverts chestnut and rump brownish-grey or buff; these differences would hardly be detected in the field except under the most favourable circumstances. Length about 6½ ins. (16·5 cms.).

Habitat. In breeding season it frequents bushy, open ground and birch or conifer forests, commonly near rivers or other water. In winter-quarters it is found largely in cultivation, copses and bushy ground.

General Habits. Habits are said to be very like Yellowhammer's. Often about roads and tracks in Mongolia. Flocks in winter.

The call is extremely like Yellowhammer's.

Food consists of seeds of grasses and mountain-plants; young are fed with insects.

Status and Distribution. Scotland—Two.

Male Fair Isle, Shetland, Oct. 30, 1911.

Male seen Papa Westray, Orkney, Oct. 15, 1943.

The species breeds from E. Russia across Asia and Siberia to Sea of Okhotsk, and a subspecies has been described from central China; it winters south to Persia, N. India and China.

1959–1978 Three additional records

ROCK BUNTING—*Emberiza cia*

PLATE 38

The male has a *pale grey head and upper breast, marked by conspicuous black bands* above, through and below the eye: the *underparts are orange-brown*, and it has a narrow whitish wing-bar. For the rest it is much as Yellowhammer, including chestnut rump and white in outer tail-feathers. Female is duller, with head markings less sharply defined; young birds look very like young Yellowhammers except for reddish-buff, not yellowish, underparts. Length about 6¼ ins. (16 cms.).

Habitat. In the breeding season it occurs principally on rocky ground with sparse scrub or scattered trees at medium elevations in mountains, but sometimes much lower or with more trees. In winter it moves to lower levels, but keeps for the most part to similar ground.

General Habits. Flight, etc. resembles Yellowhammer. It is largely terrestrial, perching on rocks and bushes, but also at all seasons in trees where these are present, and will often sing from a tree top.

Call is a sharp "tzit", hardly distinguishable from Cirl Bunting; also a fuller, rather bubbling "tucc" becoming more of a twitter in flight "tootootooc".

Food. Mainly seeds of grasses, oats, etc.; also insects.

Status and Distribution. England—Four.

Two near Shoreham, Sussex, at end October 1902.

One seen Faversham, Kent, about Feb. 14, 1905.

One seen Dale Fort, Pembs., Aug. 15, 1958.

The race concerned, *Emberiza cia cia*, breeds in Europe from the Mediterranean north to central Germany and Roumania; also in Asia Minor and Palestine. Other races occur in N. Africa, S.E. Russia and W. Asia.

1959–1978 Two additional records

YELLOW-BREASTED BUNTING—*Emberiza aureola*

PLATE 39

Males in summer are very distinct by reason of *rich chestnut upper-parts*, black face and chin; *under-parts are bright yellow*, with some streaks on flanks, and a *narrow chestnut breast-band*. Very conspicuous is the upper wing-bar forming a broad white shoulder patch; the second wing-bar is often not visible. In flight the *white wing-patch* flashes like a Chaffinch's, the bird is Chaffinch-like in proportions, and has white in outer tail feathers. In winter most of the black on head of male is lost and back is brown with black markings. In females and to a lesser extent in immatures the effect of a very prominent broad pale eye-stripe and a much less distinct light crown-stripe is to produce a head-pattern that is almost reminiscent of Aquatic Warbler; this head-pattern, at least in breeding females, is conspicuous in flight. Females and immatures are further distinguished from e.g. Yellowhammer by slight white wing-bar sometimes showing in flight; under-parts plain yellow-buff or lightly striated. Bill of male in summer very pale horn, darker in immature; legs pale brown. Length about $5\frac{1}{2}$ ins. (14 cms.).

Habitat. In winter-quarters chiefly in open country, also scrub-covered ground. In breeding season it frequents especially willow thickets and birch scrub in marshy places and bushy meadows near streams, but also dry scrub.

General Habits. It is a gregarious bird, nesting in scattered groups and occurring in winter quarters in immense flocks. Within the last century there has been a great expansion of range from Siberia to Europe.

Call is a very quiet short Robin-like "zit" or "sip", shortened even to "zi". Song is like Ortolan's, and similarly is a little variable, "dzer-dzer-dzer-dzer-dzee-dzee-deu" or "dru-dru-dru-dru-druee-druee-dree-dree-dzid-du"; the notes are flute-like but may be blurred in latter part of the song, as if two notes were superimposed.

Food consists of seeds, rice, vegetable matter; in the breeding season, insects and larvae.

Status and Distribution. Great Britain—Eleven.

In Norfolk at Cley, Sept. 21, 1905 and Sept. 4, 1913, and near Wells, Sept. 5, 1907.

On St. Kilda, Sept. 1910.

Isle of May, Sept. 4, 1936 and one seen Sept. 18, 1957.

Five at Fair Isle, Shetland, as follows: Sept. 1907, Sept. 1909, Sept. 12–13, 1946, adult male shot July 13, 1951, immature seen and trapped Sept. 9–10, 1958.

The species breeds in W. Finland, across Russia and Siberia to Manchuria and Japan; it winters in S.E. Asia south to Malaya. There are no subspecies.

1959–1978 71 additional records

RED-HEADED BUNTING—*Emberiza bruniceps*

Plate 39

The bright chestnut or golden head (colour variable), *brilliant yellow under-parts*, greenish mantle and greenish-yellow rump of the male preclude confusion with any other species. There is no white in the tail. Female is probably not certainly separable from female Black-headed Bunting, but often has some green on the upper-parts. Length about 6 ins. (15 cms.).

Habitat. In the breeding season it is found in bushy localities of all kinds, preferably, but not necessarily, near water; thickets, reed-beds and rank weed-growth on steppes, and in hedges, and even desert scrub. In winter-quarters it occurs chiefly in cultivation.

General Habits. These are described as similar to Corn and Black-headed Buntings.

The call is a brisk "pwip".

Food is probably mainly seeds and insects.

Status and Distribution. Scotland—One.

Adult male, North Ronaldsay, Orkney, June 19, 1931. (The rather numerous occurrences in England, Scotland, Ireland and Wales since about 1950 are suspect owing to heavy and repeated importations of caged birds.)

The species breeds from the Caspian to W. China and south to S. Afghanistan; it winters in India. There are no subspecies.

1959–1978 Numerous occurrences went unrecorded owing to widespread belief that they referred to escaped cage-birds, and in 1971 the species was dropped from the official list of British birds

ROSE-BREASTED GROSBEAK—*Pheucticus ludovicianus*

PLATE 40

The male in breeding plumage is unmistakable, a *black and white* bird nearly as large as a thrush, with a *rose-red breast patch*. The head, throat, neck and mantle are black, wings black with several large white patches, rump white, tail black at rest but showing more white than black when fully spread. Below the black throat a shield-shaped patch of rose-red covers the upper breast, rest of under-parts are white; in flight the white on rump and wings is very prominent, forming a broken half-circle. The female is brown, with broad white eye-stripe, pale centre to crown, and two white wing-bars; under-parts are pale brownish-white marked with well-spaced short dark streaks; the under-wing is bright yellowish; tail lacks white. In autumn and winter the male becomes browner on head and back to a varying extent, in extreme cases the head pattern approaching that of female and with dark flecks on all body plumage, but some rose is retained on breast, and wings and tail remain black and white. Immature birds resemble females but with markings usually buff rather than white; young males have a rosy tinge on breast, and underwing coverts are rose-red as are adult's. Bill whitish and very stout, legs greyish. Length about 8 ins. (20 cms.).

Habitat. In the breeding season it is found in bushy areas, often near water, on the margin of woodland where tall trees provide song posts, also in parks and large gardens with shrubberies and trees. On passage it occurs in open woodland and copses.

General Habits. It feeds both in tree tops and close to, or on, the ground. Its deliberate actions are described as being at times almost parrot-like. Not gregarious.

Call is a frequently uttered sharp metallic "kick". Song is a pleasant fluid warble of mellow notes with a thrush-like quality.

Food includes seeds, berries, fruit and insects.

Status and Distribution. Ireland—One.

Male seen Shane's Castle, Antrim, Nov. 24, 1957.

The species breeds in N. America from British Columbia to Nova Scotia and south to Georgia and central U.S.A.; it winters in Central and S. America. There are no subspecies.

1959–1978 Six additional records

NORTHERN ORIOLE (or BALTIMORE ORIOLE)—*Icterus galbula*

PLATE 40

The male is a striking bird, smaller than a thrush, with *black head, upper back and throat, bright orange on rest of the under-parts and rump.* The tail looks mainly black at rest but the outer feathers are largely orange, the wings blackish with a white wing-bar, white-edged secondaries and an orange patch on the primary coverts near the carpal joint (angle of the wing). Females are variable, in brightest plumage sometimes approaching a faded and flecked version of male, but more normally are olive above and orange-yellow below, with a double wing-bar. Immatures are like the duller females, and resemble the female Orchard Oriole (*Icterus spurius*), which is not on British List, but which is greenish yellow below rather than orange-yellow. Both these orioles in immature plumage bear some resemblance to young or female tanager, but latter lack wing-bars and have heavier whitish bills. Length about 7½ ins. (19 cms.).

Habitat. A tree-haunting species which avoids deep forest, preferring the edges of open woodland, copses, orchards and gardens.

General Habits. It tends to keep well up in trees, although sometimes nesting quite low, and is relatively inconspicuous after song has ceased. Slightly gregarious in winter.

The call is a clear low whistled "hew-li"; alarm is a loud rattle; song is a disjointed series of rich strong whistled notes, and is not infrequent in autumn.

Food is mainly insects, especially caterpillars, but includes spiders and snails. Some fruit, berries and seeds are also eaten.

Status and Distribution. England—One.

Immature seen and trapped, Lundy, Devon, Oct. 2–4, 1958.

The species breeds in Canada from central Alberta to Nova Scotia and in U.S.A. south to Texas and Georgia; it winters from Mexico to northern S. America. There are no subspecies.

1959–1978 11 additional records

p. 147

Ad. winter *Ad. summer* *Juv.*
PIED-BILLED GREBE *(ca. 1/5)*

p. 148

Adult *Immature*
GREEN HERON *(ca. 1/5)*

p. 148

Ad. f. *Ad. m.*
AMERICAN KESTREL (*ca.* 1/3)

p. 149

Ad. dark phase *Ad. pale phase* *Juv. pale phase*
ELEONORA'S FALCON (*ca.* 1/5)

p. 150

Ad. *Imm.*
ALLEN'S GALLINULE (*ca.* 1/5)

p. 150

Ad. *Imm.*
SANDHILL CRANE (*ca.* 1/10)

p. 152
& 151

Ad. summer *Ad. winter*
WHITE-TAILED PLOVER (*ca.* 1/7)

Ad. winter *Ad. winter*
GREATER SAND PLOVER (*ca.* 1/4)

p. 153
& 154

Ad. summer in flight *Immature in flight*
Ad. winter
Ad. summer
LAUGHING GULL (*ca.* 1/6)

Imm. in flight
Ad. winter in flight
Ad. summer
FRANKLIN'S GULL (*ca.* 1/6)

p. 156 & 155

Ad. winter *Ad. summer* *Imm.*
RING-BILLED GULL (*ca.* 1/12)

Ad. summer *Imm.*
SLENDER-BILLED GULL (*ca.* 1/12)

p. 157

PALLID SWIFT (*ca.* 1/5)

LITTLE SWIFT (*ca.* 1/5)

p. 161
& 158

Ad. BROWN THRASHER (*ca.* ⅕) *Ad. m.* *Imm.* YELLOW-BELLIED SAPSUCKER (*ca.* ¼)

p. 159

Ad. *Ad.* BIMACULATED LARK (*ca.* ¼) *Ad.* *Ad.* CALANDRA LARK (*ca.* ¼)

p. 160

OLIVE-BACKED PIPIT *Ad.* (*ca.* ½)

p. 162
& 163

Ad. m. *Imm.*
SIBERIAN RUBYTHROAT (*ca.* ⅓)

Ad. m.
EYE-BROWED THRUSH (*ca.* ⅓)

p. 163
& 162

Ad.
VEERY (*ca.* ¼)

Ad.
HERMIT THRUSH (*ca.* ⅖)

p. 165
& 164

Ad.
RIVER WARBLER (*ca.* ⅖)

Ad.
FAN-TAILED WARBLER (*ca.* ⅖)

p. 166 & 167

Imm. *Ad. m. summer*
SPECTACLED WARBLER (*ca.* ½)

Ad.
DESERT WARBLER (*ca.* ½)

p. 167

Ad. f. *Ad. m. summer*
RÜPPELL'S WARBLER (*ca.* ½)

p. 169
& 168

Imm. *Ad.*
PENDULINE TIT (*ca.* ½)

Ad.
SHORT-TOED TREECREEPER (*ca.* ½)

p. 170
& 171

Ad. f. *Ad. m.*
SPANISH SPARROW (*ca.* ⅖)

Ad. f. *Ad. m.*
TRUMPETER FINCH (*ca.* ⅖)

p. 171

Ad. f. *Ad. m.*
EVENING GROSBEAK (*ca.* ⅓)

p. 172
& 173

Ad. m. winter *Ad. m. summer*
TENNESSEE WARBLER (*ca.* ½)

Ad. m. summer *Ad. f.*
PARULA WARBLER (*ca.* ½)

p. 177
& 173

Ad. m. summer
Imm.
HOODED WARBLER (*ca.* ½)

Ad. m. summer
Ad. f.
YELLOW WARBLER (*ca.* ½)

p. 175
& 174

Ad. m. summer *Ad. f.*
BLACKPOLL WARBLER (*ca.* ½)

Ad. m. summer *Ad. f.*
CAPE MAY WARBLER (*ca.* ½)

p. 176
& 177

Ad. f. *Ad. m. summer*
AMERICAN REDSTART (*ca.* ½)

Ad.
OVENBIRD (*ca.* ½)

p. 178

Ad. m. summer *Imm. m.* *Ad. f.*
SCARLET TANAGER (*ca.* ⅖)

p. 179

Ad. m. *Imm.* *Ad. f.*
RUFOUS-SIDED TOWHEE (*ca.* ⅓)

p. 180

Ad. *Ad.*
FOX SPARROW (*ca.* ⅖) SONG SPARROW (*ca.* ⅖)

p. 181
& 182

Ad. spring
WHITE-CROWNED SPARROW (*ca.* ½)

Ad. m.
SLATE-COLOURED JUNCO (*ca.* ⅓)

p 183

Imm. *Ad. m. summer* *Ad. f.*
CRETZSCHMAR'S BUNTING (*ca.* ⅖)

p. 183

Ad. f. *Ad. m. spring*
Ad. m. winter
PALLAS'S REED BUNTING (*ca.* ½)

p. 185

Ad. f. *Ad. m. summer*
BOBOLINK (*ca.* ⅖)

PART TWO

Text: pages 147–185
Illustrations: plates 41–56 (following page 144)

Part Two consists mainly of species which occurred in Britain or Ireland for the first time between 1959 and 1978.

PIED-BILLED GREBE—*Podilymbus podiceps*

PLATE 41

Plump and stocky. Body shape and carriage of neck reminiscent of Little Grebe but size nearer Slavonian. Notably large-headed, with *heavy bill* which is deep-based and stout like chicken's and has curved upper mandible; bill yellowish grey in winter, but in summer becomes *whitish with a prominent black band* in middle. In winter plumage the colour of dull brown upper-parts and paler dingy flanks is not unlike Little Grebe and may cause confusion, but Pied-Billed has *white throat, fluffy white under-tail coverts* conspicuous when bird unalarmed and swimming high, white belly, and may show rufous tinge on front and sides of neck. In breeding plumage acquires black throat-patch (which in this country has become evident as early as January), narrow white ring round large eye, also the black band round bill. In all plumages, like Little Grebe, it lacks white wing-patch, but some secondaries are inconspicuously white-tipped. Length about 13–14 ins. (33–36 cms.).

Unobtrusive, usually keeping in or near cover. When disturbed may lower body in water, holding head high on thick neck, then crash-dive emerging in cover with only head above water surface; may also swim rapidly very low in water with back awash. Rarely seen in flight. Particularly wary and secretive in summer. Song, which has been heard in this country, a loud "cow-cow-cow-cow" rising in pitch, speed and volume.

Status and Distribution. Britain—At least six.

One (minimum) in Somerset, at Blagdon reservoir December 22, 1963, at near-by Chew Valley reservoir August 17–October 23, 1965, May 15, 1966, July 22–November 2, 1966, May 14–October 2, 1967, at Blagdon again May 14–June 5, 1968, and finally observed back at Chew Valley July 4–5, 1968.

Beaverdyke reservoir, Yorkshire, June 9—November 24, 1965.

Welney, Norfolk, November 9–12, 1968.

Carlingwark Loch, Kirkcudbright, October 1–8, 1975.

Loch of Strathbeg, Aberdeen, January 9–March 27, 1977.

Gouthwaite reservoir, Yorkshire, April 23–May 15, 1977.

Breeds over most of N. and S. America from Hudson Bay southwards. Few winter north of southern U.S.A. except in coastal areas.

GREEN HERON—*Butorides striatus*

PLATE 41

A diminutive heron, not much larger than Little Bittern. Can look *very dark*. Bluish-green body, rich chestnut neck with broken white streak down the front, black crown. It appears equally dark in flight (whereas spread wing of Little Bittern shows a large area of pale buff). The immature has greyer neck and upper-parts, with bands of white spots on wing-coverts; the under-parts are greyish-white, strongly marked with dark streaks. Legs yellowish-grey to bright orange. Neck is thick and short for a heron; legs also short. Length about 17 ins. (43 cms.).

It inhabits ponds and streams in wooded or open country, also marshes both fresh and coastal, feeding mainly on small fish and insects. Jerks its tail when disturbed before flying a short distance with deliberate crow-like action. Usual call "skyow".

Status and Distribution. England—One.

Near St. Austell, Cornwall, October 27, 1889.

Breeds in America from S.E. Canada south to Panama; migratory in northern part of range. Other races occur in S. America, Africa, S. Asia and Australia.

AMERICAN KESTREL—*Falco sparverius*

PLATE 42

The American counterpart of our Kestrel; male is more brightly, patchily and contrastingly coloured. Prominent white cheeks and throat, with vertical black stripes on each side of cheeks, black spot on sandy back of head, chestnut-red patch in centre of dark crown, give the male's *head a unique piebald appearance*; mantle is chestnut, barred black (not spotted like Kestrel), tail strikingly clean chestnut (not grey) with broad dark band at end, wings blue-grey (not chestnut). Female has similar head pattern to male's but otherwise is substantially like our Kestrel. Length about 9–12 ins. (23–30 cms.).

A bird of open or thinly wooded country where trees, poles, wires, cliffs, buildings provide perches. Similar in habits to Kestrel, including frequent hovering and readiness to accept a city environment. Perched bird often jerks tail upwards. Feeds on insects, small mammals and birds. Call a high-pitched, repeated "kee" or "killy".

Status and Distribution. Britain—Two.

A male Fair Isle, Shetland, May 25–27, 1976.

A female Bodmin Moor, Cornwall, June 13 to about June 28, 1976.

Breeds in most of N. and S. America, very few remaining in Canada in winter.

ELEONORA'S FALCON—*Falco eleonorae*

PLATE 42

In size between Hobby and Peregrine, but its proportions are closer to Hobby; it lacks the very solid, powerful look provided by Peregrine's breadth of chest and broad-based wings which can appear stiff, while it is more slender-looking than Hobby, with relatively longer and narrower wings; it is longer-tailed than either species. Dimorphic, but pale form is the more numerous; pale adult has general resemblance to Hobby but with distinctive under-wing pattern (considerably darker than tone of underbody and thus unlike other falcons), arising from dark under-wing coverts and dark-ended flight feathers with pale bases, producing effect of wholly *dark under-wing crossed lengthwise by a pale bar* running along centre of wing; in addition it has less sharply contrasting dark and pale head markings, and under-tail coverts usually paler than body. Dark morph adult can be confused with male Red-footed Falcon, but is larger, has uniformly dark slate-black upper-parts (not paler grey on flight feathers), has pale band along otherwise uniformly sooty under-wing, and lacks red on legs, thighs and under-tail coverts. Immatures are browner than pale phase adults, and in flight have more whitish on centre of under-wing, but show dark trailing edge throughout length of wing, and darkish under-wing coverts contrast with paler underbody. Sexes similar. Legs yellow. Length about 15 ins. (38 cms.).

Colonial, nesting almost entirely on coastal cliffs and breeding late so that young may be fed on birds passing on autumn migration; otherwise food is mainly insects taken principally on the wing. In summer immatures one or two years old may wander widely, but rarely far north of Mediterranean. Flight very agile, also soars on flat wings, and glides slowly on up-currents. Calls harsh.

Status and Distribution. England—One, Formby, Lancashire, August 8–9, 1977.

Breeds in Mediterranean area and N.W. Africa, and winters mainly in Madagascar.

ALLEN'S GALLINULE—*Porphyrula alleni*

PLATE 43

Smaller and slighter than Moorhen, with greenish-blue frontal shield and bill, and red legs. Body and wings mainly *irridescent dark green above*, and purplish-blue below and over shoulders, but head and tail nearly black. No white along flanks (unlike Moorhen), but white outer under-tail coverts like Moorhen. Young bird is mottled brown above, sandier below, but unlike the rather greyer young Moorhen lacks pale flecked line on flanks; it thus somewhat resembles young American Purple Gallinule, but latter has all-white under-tail coverts (Allen's has *dark division in centre*) and yellowish bill-tip and dull yellow legs (Allen's brownish). Length about 10 ins. (25 cms.).

It frequents swamps, backwaters and water margins with plenty of cover, swimming or often walking on floating vegetation, jerking tail like Moorhen. Legs droop in flight. Can be very secretive.

Status and Distribution. England—One, at sea off Hopton, Suffolk, January 1, 1902.

Breeds in most of Africa south of Sahara: migrates away from areas affected by dry season, when may wander widely.

SANDHILL CRANE—*Grus canadensis*

PLATE 43

Rather similar in size and appearance to the Crane of Europe, but more uniformly grey. Distinctive feature is *red forehead and crown* (in European Crane red is restricted to small inconspicuous patch on top of crown). It has whitish cheeks and chin, otherwise is grey from head to tail, *showing no black when on the ground* (European bird has mainly black head and neck with white streak up side of neck to eye, and blackish feathers drooping over tail). Juvenile is featureless, brownish, usually smaller and slimmer than similar plumaged young Crane. In both species flight-feathers are blackish at all ages, and both jerk the wings upwards on the upstroke in flight. Length about 40–45 ins. (102–114 cms.).

Inhabits open grasslands and marshes, and will accept an admixture of scattered scrub pines. Voice said to differ from Crane's, but both species give trumpeting "kroo" calls, also goose-like notes.

Status and Distribution. Ireland—One, Galley Head, Co. Cork, September 14, 1905.

Breeds from arctic N. America south to Florida, Cuba; is only a summer visitor to most of its breeding area.

GREATER SAND PLOVER—*Charadrius leschenaultii*

PLATE 44

A small plover, rather larger than Ringed Plover, and with something of that bird's thickset build. Plumage rather featureless in autumn and winter when upper-parts dull sandy-grey (immatures with slight scolloping due to narrow paler margins to feathers); off-white below, with broad band at sides of breast (not meeting across the centre) much the same colour as upper-parts; head with variable amount of whitish on forehead and cheeks, crown as mantle or more rufous; wing in flight shows pale greyish or whitish wing-bar with slightly broken edges, having a ragged darker line above it slightly darker than rest of wing. Tail same general colour as upper-parts, but white at sides (particularly of base). The whole bird is rather drab, both on ground and in flight. Large dark eye. In summer breast is cinnamon below white chin and throat, lower under-parts white; forehead white outlined by black, and broad black patch surrounds eye and ear-coverts; upper-parts more rufous than in winter, especially on sides of crown and nape. Legs greenish-yellow to drab olive-grey. Black bill is important feature, *notably bulky* for a plover, being *long also bulbous towards the tip*. Length about 8½ ins. (21·5 cms.).

Very difficult to separate from Mongolian Plover (*Charadrius mongolus*) on plumage, but latter (7 ins.) is smaller, near size of Ringed Plover, and in particular has a slighter and shorter bill.

In winter is a bird of mud- and sand-flats, chiefly coastal; rather pugnacious, bickering with horizontal back, head lowered, short-necked, burly-looking, and often calling "tree" repeated several times with trilling effect. Parental alarm notes include "klup" and "kreep".

Status and Distribution. England—One, Pagham, Sussex, December 9, 1978–January 1, 1979.

Breeds Turkey, Jordan, central Asia east to Mongolia, and winters from Egypt, Kuwait, south to Australia.

WHITE-TAILED PLOVER—*Chettusia leucura*

PLATE 44

An elegant, tall-standing plover. Body size and proportions approach those of Lapwing, with legs considerably longer and *bright yellow*. In flight the wing pattern, with heavy black expanse of blunt primaries and broad white band covering secondaries and extending forward almost to carpal joint, is not unlike Spur-winged Plover's. The completely *unmarked white tail* is unique, and legs protrude well beyond it. At rest the black and white appearance disappears, and it lacks noticeable pattern. The upper-parts are the colour of damp sand with a faint greyish-mauve tinge which intensifies on the breast and deepens to coffee-chestnut on lower breast. Head and neck considerably paler than body, especially on forehead and cheeks, and a hint of whitish streak over eye. The folded wing shows a narrow horizontal white line near its lower edge. Length about 11 ins. (27–28 cms.).

Frequents moist margins and shallow water of open, rather thinly vegetated pools and marshes. Often conspicuous. Appears almost to stand on its head when feeding, owing to length of legs. When bird is alerted carriage becomes more upright, with neck stretched up vertically. Alarm call a repeated, high-pitched "ker-wirrah", contact note a more conversational "kee-vik".

Status and Distribution. England—One, Packington, Warwickshire, July 12–18, 1975.

Breeds Aral-Caspian area, Iran, Iraq and S. Turkey, wintering mainly N. India, Persian Gulf, Egypt.

LAUGHING GULL—*Larus atricilla*

PLATE 44

A dark gull at all ages, in size between Black-headed and Common Gull, with rather long and stout bill and narrow, pointed wings. Adult has mantle and wings slate-grey, almost as Lesser Black-backed Gull, merging gradually to *black at the wing-tips* which lack white tips or spots ("mirrors") near the end of outer primaries; but the wings have a continuous white trailing edge. The white tips of the secondaries form a *white crescent on the closed wing*, curving up over the base of the primaries. Head in summer is black with white eye-ring; in winter is white with dark mottling coalescing as a noticeable spot on ear-coverts and often extending over the back of the crown as a dusky band, giving capped appearance. Bill and legs deep red in summer, duskier in winter. First year immature is featureless drab grey-brown above (darkest on primaries), and head, *neck and breast are as dark brown as rest of plumage*, distinguishing it from other gulls; in the air shows white trailing edge to wing, conspicuous white rump, and black band at end of tail as broad as in young Common Gull. In second year, breast becomes whiter, forehead paler, the black tail-band is lost, and is easily confused with young Franklin's Gull which however is smaller and shorter-billed. Length about 16 ins. (40–41 cms.).

Predominantly a coastal bird; feeds on fields as well as in tidal areas, and will bathe in fresh water, but usually not far inland. Call "ha-ha-ha".

Status and Distribution. Britain and Ireland—Nineteen. Widely scattered round coasts of England, also four Scotland and one each Wales and Ireland. Has been seen in most months of the year; adult and immature plumages.

Breeds mainly in eastern N. America, from Canada to Mexico; a partial migrant, present only in summer north of South Carolina.

FRANKLIN'S GULL—*Larus pipixcan*

PLATE 44

A North American gull, smaller, dumpier, and much shorter-legged than Laughing Gull. Adult in summer plumage resembles Laughing Gull in having black head, slate-grey mantle and inner wings (much darker than Common Gull), but has white tips to black of outer wing, and is further distinguished at all seasons by having *translucent white wing bar* (visible from both above and below) across primaries, sharply separating the black subterminal portion from the grey mid- and inner-wing; tail pale grey in centre. Both species when adult have head black in summer, and mainly white in winter but dusky behind and in front of eyes and over rear part of crown; blackish bill; at all ages in flight show a white margin on rear edge of wing. Immature differs from 1st year Laughing Gull in having pale forehead and breast, but immature Laughing in 2nd year becomes similarly whitish on forehead and breast. Accordingly, to identify a young Franklin's, it is always necessary to *establish size*: compared with Black-headed Gull it is smaller (but not as small as Little Gull), stands lower on shorter legs, and bill shorter and slimmer, whereas Laughing is larger than Black-headed (almost size of Common Gull), stands higher than either on long blackish legs, and has slightly larger bill. Length about 14 ins. (35–36 cms.).

Birds in this country have visited coastal areas, grassland and freshwater.

Status and Distribution. England—Five.

Adult, Langstone Harbour, Hampshire, February 21–May 16, 1970.

Adult, Arlington Reservoir, Sussex, July 4, 1970.

Immature, West Runton, Norfolk, October 29, 1976.

Adult, North Gare, Cleveland, July 24, 1977.

Immature, Lowestoft, Suffolk, November 13, 1977–March 27, 1978.

Breeds inland on prairie pools of Canada and central U.S.A., wintering mainly on Pacific coast of S. America. Even on migration it is rare on the Atlantic coast of N. America.

SLENDER-BILLED GULL—*Larus genei*

PLATE 45

Marginally larger than Black-headed Gull, and with many plumage similarities, but always separable on structure. The Slender-bill's *bill is about 40 per cent longer, and slightly stouter*, than Black-headed's, with downward curve towards end of upper mandible; its face tapers forwards towards the bill, accentuating bill length and making *head appear elongated* with a flatter forehead and shallower crown than that of the rounder-headed Black-headed Gull. The forward projection of head and bill is further emphasised in flight by long thin neck and long-looking tail, both particularly noticeable when drooped on landing. On the water the long neck often tends to be tilted forward, as if head were heavy. On the ground it stands taller than Black-headed, with longer legs as well as neck. Immature plumage, including wing pattern, is closely similar to young Black-headed Gull in winter, but Slender-bill has less distinct grey ear-spot and eye-mark, and on the wing the dark markings on secondaries and coverts appear paler, faded. Adult in summer can appear nearly white, having *pure white head with blackish-red bill, pale eye*, ofter a rosy tinge on under-parts, and mantle paler grey than adult Black-headed which it resembles in other respects including wing-pattern. In winter Slender-billed usually acquires a greyish spot on ear-coverts, increasing its resemblance to Black-headed. Length about 17 ins. (43 cms.).

It is mainly a bird of low-lying coasts, estuaries and lagoons, feeding in salt or brackish water, but can occur far inland in W. Asia. In this country Black-headed Gulls have generally been present at the places where it has been found.

Status and Distribution. England—Three or four.

Immature, Langney Point, Sussex, June 19—July 10, 1960.

Immature, Rye Harbour, Sussex, April 28, 1963.

Adult, Dungeness, Kent, July 21–September 12, 1971 (with gaps) and an adult (perhaps the same bird) at Minsmere, Suffolk, August 15, 1971.

Breeds in W. Asia, S. Russia, Mauretania, a few pairs in S.W. Spain, and perhaps erratically in S. France. Winters S.W. Asia and Mediterranean, southwest to Canaries and Mauretania.

RING-BILLED GULL—*Larus delawarensis*

PLATE 45

Takes the place of Common Gull in eastern North America. Adult and immature plumages of the two species are substantially similar, separation depending on small points best verified by direct comparison. In adults, the Ring-billed's grey mantle and wings are *noticeably paler grey* than in Common, closer to Black-headed Gull's; *eye is yellow*, the colour often hard to determine but always unlike the prominent black "dove-like" eye of Common Gull; the *bill is clear yellow, with a conspicuous*, fairly broad, *black band* near tip, but Common sometimes has a rather similar band; the legs can appear much yellower than the grey-green of Common, but are sometimes the same colour. Ring-billed is a larger, bulkier bird (but nevertheless closer to Common than Herring Gull in size), with flatter crown and more angular head; bill a little longer and thicker than Common's, and legs slightly longer. First winter birds have darker secondaries and cleaner, paler, greyer coverts, producing a more sharply contrasted upperwing pattern than in Common Gull of same age, and the darker secondaries' bar is also visible from underside of wing. On the other hand, young Ring-billed's tail is greyer, less white, than Common's, and the broad blackish band near end of tail often has a blurred or flecked leading edge, not sharply defined like Common. Length about 17–18 ins. (43–46 cms.).

Habits resemble those of Common Gull, and it has similar high-pitched calls. It feeds on beaches, ploughland, refuse-tips.

Status and Distribution. Britain—Twenty-two records between March 1973 and December 1978, covering most months of the year. Mainly Glamorgan, but one Aberdeenshire, one N.E. England, and four English south coast.

Breeds across southern Canada and northern U.S.A. Large numbers winter on Atlantic coast of U.S.A. south to Mexico, also inland and on Pacific coast.

PALLID SWIFT—*Apus pallidus*

PLATE 45

Difficult to separate from Swift in silhouette against the sky, but distinctive enough in direct comparison under favourable conditions viewed from above or against a background. It is distinctly paler, a *matt mousey grey-brown both above and below*, with slightly darker flight- and tail-feathers, and the white on its throat is more apparent. In size and outline it is virtually indistinguishable from Swift, but head is a little broader. Wing-beats rather slower. Length about 6½ ins. (16·5 cms.).

Behaviour is similar to Swift, and it will nest in close colonies. Call readily confused with that of Swift but is less harsh, less drawn out, "see-oh" rather than "swee-er".

Status and Distribution. England—One.

Stodmarsh, Kent, May 13–21, 1978.

Breeds in most countries bordering the Mediterranean, also N.W. Africa, the Atlantic Islands and S.W. Asia. Apparently winters mainly in tropical Africa north of equator.

LITTLE SWIFT—*Apus affinis*

PLATE 45

A small swift about size of House Martin, and like that bird has a conspicuous *broad white rump*. Otherwise plumage generally resembles common Swift, but with blacker upper-parts, blackish under-body and slightly paler under-wing; white chin patch clearer, larger, more sharply defined; fore-head pale, grey-flecked. Pale feathering at leading edge of wing is hard to see except in low-level head-on flight. *Tail is square-ended*, not forked like other swifts, and rather short, giving truncated effect. The sickle wing shape is not so elon-gated as in Swift, and it has more *rapid, fluttering wing action*. Length 5 ins. (13 cms.).

Normally gregarious, nesting mainly in buildings. Usually flies well up in air, but occasionally comes low and will drink from pool in flight. Call a rapid, high-pitched, thin, tremulous twitter.

A species which might possibly cause confusion (but has not yet occurred in Britain) is White-rumped Swift *Apus caffer*, which however is slightly larger, has a much narrower white rump-bar, and a longer, clearly forked tail.

Status and Distribution. Britain and Ireland—Two.

Cape Clear, Co. Cork, June 12, 1967.

Llanrwst, Denbighshire, November 6–7, 1973.

Breeds in much of Africa (including N. Africa) and Asia north to Syria, east to China; apparently largely resident.

YELLOW-BELLIED SAPSUCKER—*Sphyrapicus varius*

PLATE 46

A North American woodpecker, slightly smaller than Great Spotted. Adults have bright *red forehead* and front of crown, red also (in males only) on chin and throat where females are white; otherwise the sexes are similar. The *throat patch is surrounded by a black band*. Below this the under-parts are whitish with a yellow wash; flanks dark-streaked. The head, except where red, is boldly banded or striped with black and white; back is more softly and narrowly barred blackish and whitish, as are primaries. Remainder of wing black, with a long white stripe conspicuous on closed wing. Immature shows the same long white wing-stripe, but is mainly dark greyish-brown above and below, with paler mottlings or spots which are particularly evident on the back; on the head a buff streak runs back from eye and another from base of bill down to side of neck. Length 8–8½ ins. (20–21 cms.).

An inconspicuous bird of well-wooded country and orchards, often attacking bark to make sap exude, but feeds mainly on insects. Voice a whining cat-like mew.

Status and Distribution. England—One, immature, Tresco, Scilly Isles, September 26–October 6, 1975.

Breeds from Alaska across central Canada to Newfoundland and Georgia; winters from U.S.A. to Panama.

CALANDRA LARK—*Melanocorypha calandra*

PLATE 46

A large heavy lark with stout bill, and characteristic black patch at side of neck. Upper-parts greyish with dark streaks, and like many larks it has a pale buffish stripe over eye. Under-parts mainly white, with a *large black patch on each side of base of neck*, not meeting across breast which is buffish with dark flecks. No crest. It is more distinctive in flight; when over-head the white underbody contrasts with *wings, which appear black* apart from *conspicuous white trailing edge*; wings often look pointed, triangular, in circling song-flight. When flying low over ground, the white tips of secondaries and inner primaries are noticeable; otherwise upper-wing is medium grey near leading edge, the remainder darker. Tail is black-brown, without white tip, but *white outer feathers* give it white sides. See also Bimaculated Lark. Length about 7½ ins. (19 cms.).

A bird of arid or stony open plains and steppe, especially cornlands and dry grassland. Tends to flock in winter, often loosely colonial in summer. Sings circling at considerable height, also low down in curious, slow, hanging flight, and on ground. Calls often nasal, jangling; one note has been written "trrrreeeep".

Status and Distribution. Britain—Two.

Portland Bill, Dorset, April 2, 1961.

Fair Isle, Shetland, April 28, 1978.

Breeds Mediterranean Europe, N. Africa and mid-Asia east to Iran, Afghanistan. Partial migrant, but does not extend far south of breeding range in winter.

BIMACULATED LARK—*Melanocorypha bimaculata*

PLATE 46

Has general resemblance to Calandra Lark, but is paler and browner (less grey), sometimes looking sandy-chestnut; dark streaks on upper-parts are little evident on nape and rump. Unlike Calandra, *has no white on wing in flight*, no white along sides of tail; tail however is *white-tipped* (again unlike Calandra), the white at end of each feather forming a ragged-edged band. Is also slightly smaller than Calandra, has a shorter tail (noticeable in flight), a long whitish stripe over eye a little more evident than Calandra's, and may show creamy, slightly irregular, braces over shoulders. A black band across the lower throat may be broad at centre, tappering towards side of neck, but its shape can vary, for example it may not meet at centre of breast, and may appear to fork at ends, one prong running up side of neck. No crest, but crown feathers can be raised. In flight, under-wing coverts dark, but primaries and secondaries are pale, sometimes appearing almost translucent (blackish in Calandra); short, rounded wings, with plump body low-slung. Length about 6½ ins. (16·5 cms.).

An upland bird, frequenting stony, rather barren slopes and hills; generally at higher altitude than Calandra, but where overlap occurs Calandra chooses flatter, more vegetated (often arable) ground for breeding. Usually not shy. Voice resembles Calandra; will sing high in air, from low perch like dead thistle, or on a stone. Calls include "chirrp".

Status and Distribution. Britain—Three.

Lundy Island, Devon, May 7–11, 1962.

St. Mary's, Scilly Isles, October 24–27, 1975.

Fair Isle, Shetland, June 8, 1976.

An Asiatic species, breeding from Turkey to Afghanistan and north to about 50° in central U.S.S.R. In winter extends south to N.E. Africa and N.W. India.

OLIVE-BACKED PIPIT—*Anthus hodgsoni*

PLATE 47

One of the easiest pipits to identify, with short, startling supercilium, a *black ear-spot*, and black breast-spotting; about size of Tree Pipit. Back uniform-looking olive-green (not brown), contrasting markedly with under-parts which are clean white on underbody, washed yellowish on throat and breast; heavily spotted black on breast becoming more thinly streaked on flanks. Crown colour like back but flecked black; a black line above supercilium. The supercilium is short and broad, *strikingly white* above and behind eye, orange-buff in front of it. A dark eyestripe separates the rear end of the supercilium from *a drop-shaped downward extension* which is as white as the supercilium itself. Below this white drop in the region of the ear-coverts is a black spot at the rear margin of olive-brown cheek. Whitish outer tail-feathers, and two inconspicuous wing-bars. Length about 6 ins. (15 cms.).

A shy, tree-loving bird, feeding on ground among trees or near forest edge; when disturbed flies up calling, to take cover in tree canopy. Pumps tail vigorously and habitually, like a wagtail. Voice recalls Tree Pipit's note, sometimes that of Richard's Pipit.

Status and Distribution. Britain—Twelve.

The occurrences extend from Fair Isle to Scilly Isles, and from west Wales to Norfolk; two in April–May, the remainder autumn from late September to late November. The first record was on Skokholm Is., Wales, April 14, 1948; the others 1964–1978.

Breeds from N.E. Europe to Japan, and winters in S.E. Asia.

BROWN THRASHER—*Toxostoma rufum*

PLATE 46

A somewhat thrush-like bird with *long, curved-looking bill.* Body size like that of a slender Song Thrush, but tail almost as long as body, making overall length as great as Mistle Thrush. *Upper-parts bright reddish-brown,* slightly darker on forehead; cheeks greyer and paler; two conspicuous whitish wing-bars, no white in tail. Under-parts are white or off-white, throat unmarked, the remainder with bold thrush-like spots or streaks. Eye bright yellow. Sexes similar. Length about 11 ins. (28 cms.).

Keeps in or close to cover of dry thickets, shrubby areas and open woodland with brambles and other tangles. Feeds usually low down on insects, berries, or scratches among fallen leaves and hammers acorns and seeds. Unobtrusive rather than shy, flitting short distances, often cocking or thrashing its tail. Call a harsh, sudden "chack", fairly frequent; song rich and melodious.

Status and Distribution. England—One near Swanage, Dorset, November 18, 1966–February 5, 1967.

Breeds eastern and mid-U.S.A. and S.E. Canada, wintering mainly in south and south-east U.S.A.

SIBERIAN RUBYTHROAT—*Luscinia calliope*

PLATE 47

The size of a Nightingale with some characteristics of Bluethroat. Warm olive-brown above, rather more rufous on rump, and rufous fringes of secondaries make a panel on closed wing. Tail rather long, unpatterned. Male has a white stripe from forehead over eye; another white stripe runs back from base of lower mandible along bottom of cheek. Between these stripes a dark patch from base of bill to ear-coverts surrounds most of white-ringed eye. Main feature is *rich ruby-red chin and throat*, margined by a blackish line which below the throat merges into grey breast; buffer on flanks and lower breast, belly white. Female has throat dull white, breast and flanks buffish brown; whitish stripe from bill over eye, becoming obscure behind eye. Dark line through eye; upper-parts as male. Young male resembles female but has some tinges of red on throat. Length about 6¼ ins. (16 cms.).

A bird of thick, low cover, often near water; reluctant to show itself; feeds mainly on ground. Long-legged; often cocks tail, will bob like Robin, and droop wings. Calls include a plaintive "chee-vee" and a harsh rattle of alarm; sings well at dusk in breeding season.

Status and Distribution. Britain—Two.

Fair Isle, Shetland, October 9–11, 1975.

Donna Nook, Lincolnshire, October 14, 1977.

Breeds across north-central Asia from Urals to Pacific, and winters in S.E. Asia.

HERMIT THRUSH—*Catharus guttatus*

PLATE 48

A small American thrush, about size of Corn Bunting. Olive-brown crown, back and wings contrast with distinctive *chestnut-brown rump and tail*. Under-parts dull white, clouded buffish on sides of breast, well spotted or streaked with dark brown on breast and flanks, fading out towards belly. Narrow buff-white eye-ring. The plumage pattern and breast-spotting is reminiscent of Song Thrush, as is the general coloration of under-parts, also upper-parts with the exception of rufous rump and tail which is special feature of Hermit. Moreover, Song Thrush is appreciably larger. See also Fox Sparrow. Length about 7 ins. (18 cms.).

A retiring bird, frequenting moist woods especially if including conifers, swampy thickets, also dry bushgrown hills; seldom in really open country except sometimes on migration. Often cocks tail slowly. Calls include low "chuck" and a mewing note. Breeding song of beautiful pure cadences.

Status and Distribution. Scotland—One Fair Isle, Shetland, June 2, 1975.

Breeds from Newfoundland to Alaska and south to north-east U.S.A. and California; winters from central U.S.A. to Guatemala.

VEERY—*Catharus fuscescens*

PLATE 48

Another small American thrush, about size of Hermit Thrush. *All upper-parts including wings and tail uniform rusty cinnamon*, redder-brown than any other thrush on our list. Upper breast buff, lightly marked with indistinct brown spots which run up sides of throat but do not extend to lower breast or down buffish flanks; remaining under-parts whitish. No eye-ring visible in the field. Length about 7 ins. (18 cms.).

Normally shy and cover-loving, chiefly haunting damp deciduous woodland with plentiful undergrowth; feeds mainly on ground. Call a quiet "phew", descending in pitch, helpful when known in finding and identifying the bird.

Status and Distribution. England—One, Porthgwarra, Cornwall, October 6, 1970.

Breeds from Newfoundland across southern Canada, also in U.S.A. mainly in the north. Winters in S. America.

EYE-BROWED THRUSH—*Turdus obscurus*

PLATE 47

A small thrush about size of Redwing, and with some similarities of appearance, but immediately separated by *lack of spots or streaks on breast*. Upper-parts are olive-brown, with head and neck often rather greyer in males. A conspicuous *white eye-stripe*, and males sometimes have another white area below and forward of the eye. Grey from sides of neck extends as a band across throat in well marked males, in others this is narrow or absent; also absent in females which have white throats, streaked dark at the sides. *Flanks and sides of breast warm apricot,* but ranging from rich dark orange in some males to buffish in the dullest females, the colour usually meeting (and fading somewhat) across the front of the breast in both sexes; no streaks or spots. Remainder of under-parts pure white, including under-tail coverts. Some yellow at base of bill. Immature resembles female but has slight pale bar across folded wing. Length about 8–9 ins. (20–23 cms.).

A thrush-like bird, despite lack of spotting. Will cock head to one side when feeding on ground. In winter frequents wooded and more open country, solitary or flocking like Redwing, and has some similar call notes.

Status and Distribution. Britain—Four.
Oundle, Northamptonshire, October 5, 1964.
North Rona, Outer Hebrides, October 16, 1964.
St. Agnes, Scilly Isles, December 5, 1964.
Lochwinnoch, Renfrewshire, October 22, 1978.
Breeds in central and east Siberia, wintering in S.E. Asia.

FAN-TAILED WARBLER—*Cisticola juncidis*

PLATE 48

A very small, stubby-tailed warbler, only slightly larger than a Wren; tawny-coloured with streaked back, recalling Aquatic Warbler. Crown is pale brown with narrow dark streaks forming distinct lines; the back is much the same colour but the streaks are broader, farther apart and more broken. Short, rounded wing lacks wing-bar or other pronounced feature. Rump unstreaked chestnut-buff. The graduated tail is brown, darkening towards end on the upper surface, and *tipped white.* On the underside the white feather tips are preceded by a crisply defined band of black, so when tail is fanned and cocked it appears from behind to be fringed by a semi-circle of black and white spots. Under-parts whitish, with a warm tawny wash on breast and flanks. Sexes similar. Length about 4 ins. (10 cms.).

A bird of low cover in open country, frequenting edges of cornfields, waste grasslands and areas of rushes (not reeds), generally avoiding trees. Normally skulking, but very evident in *bouncing song-flight* well up in air, giving repeated, penetrating "dzeep" notes. Also calls "teu" and "zip", perched or in flight.

Status and Distribution. England and Ireland—Three.

Cape Clear, Co. Cork, April 23, 1962.

Norfolk, at Cley, August 24 and Holme, August 29–September 5, 1976.

In song, Lodmoor, Dorset, June 24–28, 1977.

Breeds S. Europe, much of Africa, S. Asia east to Japan, N. Australia. Has recently spread from Mediterranean Europe up west coast of France to Channel coast. Mainly sedentary, hard-hit by severe winters.

RIVER WARBLER—*Locustella fluviatilis*

PLATE 48

Difficult to observe except when singing, like Grasshopper and other *Locustella* warblers. It is distinguished by *lack of streaking on upper-parts* but has soft, clouded or *blurred spots or streaks on throat and upper breast.* Upper-parts are dark earth-brown, rather warmer on wings and tail-coverts; under-parts off-white with buff wash, but slightly darker grey-brown on flanks and sides of breast. Very faint buff stripe over eye. Legs pink. Sexes similar. Length about 5 ins. (13 cms.).

Some related warblers can cause confusion. Grasshopper Warbler has strongly streaked (almost chequered) upper-parts with yellowish tinge, but under-parts rather similar to River Warbler; Lanceolated and Pallas's Grasshopper Warblers (which see) also have streaked upper-parts; Savi's Warbler has upper-parts unstreaked and warmer brown, but breast also unstreaked. All have well-rounded tails, like River Warbler.

Cover-loving, skulking and hard to flush, generally frequenting damp areas and keeping to bushy cover, often below trees. Breeding birds best located by distinctive song, basically similar to Grasshopper Warbler's but immediately recognisable by slower tempo of the clicks forming the reeling song, so that components are not run together into a purr, but are a series of just-separated notes "chi-chi-chi- . . ." sounding like a very rapid stutter, which may continue unbroken for a couple of minutes; often delivered from exposed perch on top of bush or bare branch low in tree.

Status and Distribution. Britain—Three.

Fair Isle, Shetland, September 24–25, 1961.

Another there on September 16, 1969.

Bardsey Island, Caernarvonshire, September 17, 1969.

Breeds from Germany, N. Balkans and Baltic States eastwards to W. Siberia; winters in E. Africa.

SPECTACLED WARBLER—*Sylvia conspicillata*

PLATE 49

Male in spring is reminiscent of Whitethroat in plumage pattern, but is smaller, more dainty, has less strident, scratchy song, and is more noticeably coloured with darker grey head, blacker face, *richer pink breast* (the last two features making white throat more conspicuous), mantle greyer, less brown (so that *rufous wing-patch* stands out more prominently), and bright, pale, *translucent-looking straw-coloured legs*. Female has paler head, less colour on breast. In autumn, immature is readily confused with very similar young Subalpine Warbler (see below); Sardinian Warbler females and immatures must also be eliminated; they are much darker, bulkier (more like Barred Warbler), and have heavier bill with whitish wedge at base of lower mandible. Spectacled is a neat bird, in form more resembling Lesser Whitethroat or Subalpine Warbler than Whitethroat; immature lacks dark ear-coverts (like Subalpine and Whitethroat, unlike Lesser Whitethroat), but has rufous in wing (like Whitethroat, unlike Subalpine or Lesser Whitethroat), orange wash on flanks (like Subalpine, unlike Whitethroat or Lesser Whitethroat), and narrow white eye-ring which is inconspicuous but when seen is a good character at all ages, not shared by other species mentioned above. Length about $5\frac{1}{4}$ ins. (13·5 cms.).

A bird of rather open, dry, low scrub. Sings from exposed perch or not infrequent song flights of Whitethroat type; alarm a quiet Wren-like rattle. Does not regularly cock tail like Subalpine Warbler.

Status and Distribution. England—Two.

Spurn Point, Yorkshire, October 21–31, 1968.

Porthgwarra, Cornwall, October 17, 1969.

Breeds in N. Africa and much of Mediterranean area east to Jordan. Most winter in northern Sahara.

RÜPPELL'S WARBLER—*Sylvia rueppelli*

PLATE 49

The male is readily distinguished from other warblers by *black throat and white moustache*; otherwise is much like Sardinian Warbler, including red eye. However, Rüppell's is larger, and tail relatively shorter and squarer, while paler, *bluish or french-grey mantle* of male at once attracts attention. Female has whitish throat and greyish-brown cap (often with some black) but moustache is sufficiently indicated for identification. Outer tail-feathers white. Legs bright red-brown. Young birds much as adult, but duller. Length about 5½ ins. (14 cms.).

Breeds in thick scrub, often on rocky slopes or in gullies; at other times frequents gardens, hedges, and scrub or bushes of all sorts. Scolding note resembles Sardinian's but is harsher and louder, like two pebbles rapidly knocked together; song is similar to Sardinian's but fuller and more musical, given from perch or in heavy, zigzag display-flight with slow wing-beat and extended tail and wings, recalling display-flight of Greenfinch.

Status and Distribution. Scotland—One.

A male (singing) at Sumburgh, Shetland, August 13–September 16, 1977.

Breeds Crete, Aegean region, S. Turkey and Levant. Winters in N.E. Africa.

DESERT WARBLER—*Sylvia nana*

PLATE 49

A small, *pale, sandy-grey* warbler, smaller than Whitethroat and with more compact, less elongated, body shape but with rather long tail which is, however, proportionately shorter than Dartford Warbler's. Upper-parts uniform drab sandy-grey, including sides of head to well below eye; lower cheeks and under-parts paler, off-white with greyish tinge. Flight-feathers fringed rufous-buff. Most notable feature is *warm brown tail*, becoming more sandy chestnut or pale *foxy towards rump*; outer tail feathers white. Some birds show a white eye-ring. Immatures, and to lesser extent adults in autumn, are more rufous-tinged above. Bill fine, mainly yellowish-horn with, at least in autumn, a dark tip. Legs very pale yellowish-horn. Sexes similar. Length about 4½ ins. (11·5 cms.).

It frequents steppe and semi-desert with scattering of low bushes such as camel thorn. Often quite tame, with hardly any attempt at concealment, but sometimes skulks in centre of a bush and refuses to be flushed. When moving among low bushes, flies mainly below bush-top height which may be 2 feet or less, often landing on bare ground a foot short of a bush and continuing into it with a little run and a hop; forages largely on open ground close around bush. Sometimes slightly cocks tail. Calls include an infrequent quiet *Sylvia*-type "churr", and a rapid, high-pitched "chee-chee-chee-chee". Song has some similarities to Whitethroat's but is less powerful; may be given in similar sort of song-flight.

Status and Distribution. England—Three.

Portland Bill, Dorset, December 16, 1970–January 2, 1971.

Spurn Point, Yorkshire, October 20–24, 1975.

Frinton-on-Sea, Essex, November 20–21, 1975.

The race described, *Sylvia nana nana*, breeds in central Asia and winters from N.W. India to the Red Sea. Another race, *Sylvia nana deserti*, more golden-sandy above and whiter below, breeds in N.W. Sahara.

SHORT-TOED TREECREEPER—*Certhia brachydactyla*

PLATE 50

A most difficult bird to identify, even in the hand. On the continent of Europe, Short-toed Treecreeper is usually separable from typical Treecreeper by the former's generally duller appearance, having drabber greyer upper-parts with less obvious white spots, less distinct white streak above eye, less rufous on rump, and under-parts dingy off-white on breast becoming buff or brownish on flanks (Treecreeper being cleaner and whiter below). However, Treecreepers of the British race, *Certhia familiaris britannica*, particularly in southern England, are intermediate in all these features including having a buff wash on flanks. In addition although Short-toed has, on average, a shorter hind-claw (7·87 mm.) and a longer bill (17·65 mm.), the area of overlap of measurements of the two species is considerable. The full song of Short-toed is louder, shorter and has a more emphatic rhythm than Treecreeper, and although it has several calls virtually the same as those of Treecreeper, two of them, a Hedge Sparrow-like "zeet", and a somewhat Chaffinch-like "chink", appear to be diagnostic of

Short-toed. However, the value of voice for separation has been reduced since it has been found on the continent that both species may learn at least part of the other's song pattern. The problem of treecreeper identification has been examined with care by C. J. Mead and D. I. M. Wallace in *British Birds*, 1976 (pp. 117–131). They also measured many specimens of both species and found considerable overlap in the lengths of bill, hind-claw and wing. They conclude that only the combination of very dull plumage with an indistinct supercilium gives worthwhile cause to suspect Short-toed. The complement of an obviously long, bent bill will further indicate that species, but the absence of such does not rule it out. Separation of the two species in the field has yet to be proved possible in Britain. Length about 5 ins. (13 cms.).

Habitat differences are far from clear-cut; although on the Continent the Short-toed frequents gardens, and more often woodland, at lower altitudes, these types of terrain are already occupied by Treecreeper in this country.

Status and Distribution. England—Seven, all trapped.

Dungeness, Kent, September 27–30, 1969.
Hornsea, Yorkshire, October 26, 1970.
Worth, Kent, September 26, 1973.
Sandwich, Kent, April 4, 1974.
Epping Forest, Essex, May 26, 1975.
Two, Dungeness, Kent, October 7–10, 1978.

Breeds Channel Islands and most of continental Europe from Holland and Germany southwards; also N. Africa and Turkey. Largely resident.

PENDULINE TIT—*Remiz pendulinus*

Plate 50

Smaller than Blue Tit, but less portly and with a longer, more evident tail. Head and neck pale grey, with a prominent *black, shrike-like, eye-patch* or mask. *Mantle and wing-coverts chestnut*, paler and greyer on rump. Flight-feathers and tail blackish, margined with white. Throat white, rest of under-parts whitish washed buffish or chestnut, especially on breast and flanks. Female similar or a little duller. Juvenile lacks black on head and chestnut on upper-parts. Some Asian races have head chestnut, or even wholly blackish including throat. Length about $4\frac{1}{4}$ ins. (11 cms.).

It inhabits marshy or riverine areas, sometimes dryer localities. Mainly haunts trees or bushes such as willow, tamarisk, poplar, although it will enter reeds and in some regions breeds in reed-beds. A confiding but unobtrusive bird, often first located by frequently used, distinctive call "tsee" or "seeou", soft and plaintive but rather more substantial than somewhat similar thin note of Robin. Song sweet but very soft.

Status and Distribution. England—Two.

Spurn Point, Yorkshire, October 22–28, 1966.

St. Agnes, Scilly Isles, October 25, 1977.

Breeds in parts of south and east Europe, north to Poland and Baltic States, and eastwards across central Asia to China; range expansion north and west in central Europe in recent decades. A partial migrant.

SPANISH SPARROW—*Passer hispaniolensis*

PLATE 50

Size and build of House Sparrow. Male distinguished by extensive *black across breast, also black streaks down flanks* and over shoulders onto mantle. Head resembles Tree Sparrow's, with chestnut crown and nape, but white cheek lacks black spot of Tree. Female closely similar to female House Sparrow, but flanks faintly streaked and cheeks paler. Length about 5¾ ins. (14·5 cms.).

Gregarious. Not normally an urban bird, usually nesting in colonies in groups of trees or bushes, including groves of palms and olives; also frequents scrub. Sometimes in large flocks. May hybridise with House Sparrow. Voice more rhythmic than House Sparrow.

Status and Distribution. England—Three.

Lundy Island, Devon, June 9–about 19, 1966.

St. Mary's, Scilly Isles, October 21, 1972.

Bryher, Scilly Isles, October 22–24, 1977.

Breeds N.W. Africa, southern parts of Mediterranean Europe, and eastwards to central Asia. Largely migratory, reaching Sudan and Arabia in winter.

TRUMPETER FINCH—*Bucanetes githagineus*

PLATE 50

An unobtrusive dumpy finch, about size of Linnet but more portly, short-tailed, large-headed and with stout, short, blunt bill of Bullfinch-like proportions. Male in breeding plumage has pale greyish head, becoming more sandy-brown on back with darker wing and tail feathers; under-parts pale greyish-buff. The whole plumage has a *suffusion of pink*, especially on rump, and becoming richer, even carmine, on fringes of some feathers of forehead, wings, tail, breast and belly. *Bill bright coral-red.* Female, also male in winter, much duller with scarcely any red in plumage; rather uniform, lacking contrasts or streaking; bill yellowish. Length about 5 ins. (13 cms.).

Inhabits barren, desolate, stony or rocky (not necessarily mountainous) country, often devoid of trees or bushes. Requires access to water for drinking. Upright stance when alert or singing, but frequently crouches when feeding. Generally allows close approach, and readily overlooked as closely resembles ground on which it feeds. Calls include a variety of quiet yapping notes audible only at close range; song is slightly louder, a very distinctive sudden nasal buzz, almost a bray.

Status and Distribution. Britain—Two.

Minsmere, Suffolk, May 30–June 19, 1971.

Handa Island, Sutherland, June 8–9, 1971.

Breeds S. Spain (with recent increase), N. Africa and east to India. Apparently largely resident although flocking in winter, and some movement evidently occurs.

EVENING GROSBEAK—*Hesperiphona vespertina*

PLATE 51

In silhouette resembles Hawfinch, with massive bill, burly body, short tail, and undulating flight. Body plumage of male is mainly yellow, becoming tawny-brown on breast, mantle and cheeks. Broad yellow band on forehead running back over eye almost encloses black crown. Sharp contrast is provided by *black tail, and wings* with very prominent large *white patch* which can cover lower back of perched bird, and is visible at long range in flight. Female is mainly silver-grey, yellower on nape and flanks, silvery on rump; white on secondaries forms less intense patch than male's, and female additionally has a small white patch at base of primaries, also some white towards tips of tail feathers and primaries. Bill whitish to pale green. Length about 8 ins. (20 cms.).

A striking, gregarious bird, nesting in boreal conifer forest; seeks berries and seeds of trees, shrubs and weeds in winter when it is regular at bird-tables, partial to sunflower seed, and can become very confiding. Call a ringing "clee-ip", song a disjointed warbling.

Status and Distribution. Scotland—One.

St. Kilda, Outer Hebrides, March 26, 1969.

Breeds across Canada and in Rocky Mountains in U.S.A. A partial migrant, extending southwards in winter over most of U.S.A.

TENNESSEE WARBLER—*Vermivora peregrina*

PLATE 51

One of the large family of American wood warblers (which are not closely related to the Wood Warbler of the Old World). Many of the species are confusingly similar, especially in female, immature, or autumn plumage, requiring attention to detail such as presence or absence of wing-bars, streaks on back, white in tail, yellow on rump, also head pattern.

Tennessee male in spring has clean grey head and nape, *white stripe over dark line through eye*, white or whitish on all under-parts including chin and flanks; rather uniform greenish upper-parts (lacking wing-bar) contrast with grey head. Is separated from rather similarly plumaged Red-eyed Vireo by lack of red eye, lack of black line above white supercillary, smaller size, slender bill, and much less heavy, deliberate movements. Female in spring has greenish head and yellowish-washed under-parts. Autumn features of both sexes are greenish head and back, *pale yellowish stripe over eye*, dingy yellow under-parts, white under-tail coverts, *no streaks above or below*; a faint pale wing-bar is usually acquired. Length about 5 ins. (13 cms.).

A small, very active warbler of *Phylloscopus* size. On spring migration it keeps in tree-tops but in autumn descends to low bushes. Call a sharp "zeep-zeep".

Status and Distribution. Scotland—Two, both immatures on Fair Isle, Shetland, in 1975; one September 6–18, the other September 24.

Breeds in Canada and north U.S.A., and winters in Central America and northern South America.

PARULA WARBLER—*Parula americana*

PLATE 51

A small, colourful American warbler. Male in spring has mainly *blue upper-parts* (greenish on mantle), and *bright yellow below with mahogany breast-band* and white belly; two prominent white wing-bars. Female, male in autumn and immatures have greener, less blue, upper-parts, the dark breast-band is reduced or absent, the white wing-bars are retained. White eye-ring is bisected by thin dark eye-stripe. Length about 4½ ins. (11·5 cms.).

A restless warbler with quicker, more active feeding movements than our similar-sized but slimmer *Phylloscopus* warblers. It often shows a preference for feeding in tree-tops, and for the vicinity of swamps or water-margins. Will cling upside down, tit-like, when feeding. Call heard from a bird in England was a soft "weet".

Status and Distribution. England—Three.

Tresco, Scilly Isles, October 16–17, 1966.

St. Ives, Cornwall, November 26, 1967.

Portland, Dorset, October 9, 1968.

Breeds in eastern N. America from Gulf of Mexico into southern Canada. A migrant, wintering in south Florida, West Indies, Central America.

YELLOW WARBLER—*Dendroica petechia*

PLATE 52

An eye-catching American warbler, bright primrose or canary-*yellow* on head and all under-parts, rather darker greenish-yellow on upper-parts including hindneck; two pale yellow bars across browner wings; flight feathers are edged clean yellow. The brown tail feathers have pale *yellow inner webs* (often described confusingly as "spots" in American literature); this an important feature in autumn, eliminating somewhat similar female or immature Wilson's and Hooded Warblers. Black eye is prominent in uniform pale head. No white in plumage. Male has long, rather broad (not very conspicuous) chestnut-pink streaks on under-parts from throat to belly; these are largely or entirely absent from females and immatures. Length about 5 ins. (13 cms.).

Another quite active warbler darting in and out of sight among the foliage of bushes, thickets and shade trees which are preferred to thick woodland or high tree tops; often in moist areas in willows and alders, also gardens. Call a sharp "chip".

Status and Distribution. Wales—One.

Bardsey Island, Caernarvonshire, August 29, 1964.

Breeds in most parts of Canada and U.S.A., wintering in Central and northern South America.

CAPE MAY WARBLER—*Dendroica tigrina*

PLATE 52

In breeding plumage male is the only American warbler with *chestnut cheeks*. Under-parts bright yellow, strongly striped with black spots. Dull greenish back is also spotted or streaked with black. Rump yellow, unmarked. Wing-coverts very extensively white, forming large, mainly white, wing-patch. Females, immatures, and males in autumn and winter, are comparatively dull and need care in identification: greyish-green above without dark streaks, paler greenish-yellow rump; the sides of neck (behind ear-coverts) usually *yellow*—in autumn an indistinct but valuable feature if visible; tail dark but outer feathers have large *white patch near tip* of inner web. Under-parts pale greyish-yellow or almost white with plentiful fine dark streaking; under-tail coverts white. Two white wing-bars. No white eye-ring; faint dark eye-stripe. Legs dark. Can be confused with several other warblers in female or autumn plumage, including Yellow-rumped (which has brighter yellow rump, contrasting sharply with streaked and browner back; throat whiter than breast), Palm Warbler (with streaked brown back; yellow under-tail coverts), Pine

Warbler (dingy, without yellowish rump; very faint breast-streaks). Length about 5 ins. (13 cms.).

An insect-feeder, but with more sluggish movements than some other wood warblers. Breeds in spruce forest, and often occurs in conifers on migration. Song variable, usually half-a-dozen or so similar, high-pitched thin, sibilant notes.

Status and Distribution. Scotland—One singing at Paisley, Renfrewshire, June 17, 1977.

Breeds in Canada and north-east U.S.A., and winters in West Indies.

BLACKPOLL WARBLER—*Dendroica striata*

PLATE 52

Breeding male has *black cap down to eye level, conspicuous white cheeks*, black moustache, and strong black streaks on flanks and sides of breast; otherwise under-parts all pure white. Upper-parts olive-grey streaked black, rump uniform olive-grey; two white wing-bars. Legs pale yellow. Autumn birds are rather featureless, olive-green above with faint dark streaks on back; paler below, greenish-yellow with soft dark streaks on flanks; white under-tail coverts; two white wing-bars and pale yellowish legs. Female in summer is cleaner coloured than in autumn, whiter below and with clearer black streaks on back and flanks. In all plumages the outer tail-feathers have a large white patch on inner web near the tip (visible from below). Length about 5 ins. (13 cms.).

Readily confused in autumn with Bay-breasted Warbler which, however, has black legs, buff under-tail coverts, buffish (less yellow) breast and flanks with very faint dark streaking; throat paler than breast (no contrast in Blackpoll). Pine Warbler, also very similar, has black legs, lacks streaks on back, and only adult male has dark-streaked sides in autumn.

Blackpoll is American wood warbler most frequently observed in this country, where its calls have been described as a thin 'ssts' like flight-call of Goldcrest, and a loud "chik" like anxiety note of breeding Meadow Pipit. Feeds very actively and openly in bushes and small trees, also hovering about foliage and making agile sallies to take flying insects; will also feed in tall trees on migration.

Status and Distribution. Britain—Fifteen.

First recorded St. Agnes, Scilly Isles, October 12–25, 1968.

There have been eleven other Scilly reports (ten in October in various years, and one November 2–3), two Bardsey Island, Caernarvonshire, October 22–23, 1968, and October 7–9, 1976. One Prawle Point, Devon, September 18–29, 1976.

Breeds north-east U.S.A., and almost all Canada north to tree-limit. A longer distance migrant than most members of its family, wintering in northern South America.

AMERICAN REDSTART—*Setophaga ruticilla*

PLATE 53

A beautiful bird, readily identified in all plumages, unlike most other American wood warblers. Adult male in summer has head and body *black* except for orange-red patch on side of breast in the region of the shoulder, and white lower breast and belly; *wings black with orange-red band across base of flight feathers*; the long, large *tail is orange-red* with broad black terminal band and black central feathers. The orange patches are most conspicuous, flaunted in frequent fanning of raised tail and drooping of wings. Adult females, and males in winter or first summer plumage, have the orange-red patches replaced by bright pale yellow, giving largely similar pattern although their under-parts including throat are white, heads blue-grey (with white eye-ring), and upper-parts mainly olive-brown. Immatures in autumn are similar but duller. Length about 5–5½ ins. (13–14 cms.).

A bird of open deciduous or mixed woodland, especially along streams, passage birds occurring in less wooded areas and gardens. Very active in feeding on insects within tree-cover, also taking them on the wing in flycatcher fashion; will also feed on the ground. Call a clear, high-pitched "sweet", also "chip".

Status and Distribution. England and Ireland—Two.

Porthgwarra, Cornwall, October 21, 1967.

Cape Clear Island, Co. Cork, October 13–14, 1968.

Breeds across much of Canada, and northern and eastern U.S.A. Winters from Mexico and West Indies to northern South America.

OVENBIRD—*Seiurus aurocapillus*

PLATE 53

More portly, full-bellied, than most warblers. British observers have noted resemblances of size and stance to a Nightingale, and likened upper-parts colouration to a giant Goldcrest. Upper-parts bright olive-green, head with *orange-tan crown-stripe bordered by black*, and large black eye set in *conspicuous white eye-ring*; under-parts white or creamy, heavily streaked on breast and flanks with black spots forming blotched lines. *Legs bright pale pinkish.* Plumage similar in both sexes and at all seasons and ages (except juvenile, too young to migrate, which is brown and streaked, both above and below). Length about 6 ins. (15 cms.).

Essentially a bird of the forest floor, preferring dry, deciduous, thick woodland with some undergrowth, where it walks and feeds in the leaf litter; perches low. A bird in Shetland fed, of necessity, on open ground among rocks. Call a rather sharp chirp.

Status and Distribution. Scotland—One. Out Skerries, Shetland, October 7–8, 1973.

Breeds central and south-eastern Canada, and central and eastern U.S.A. Winters West Indies, Central America and northern South America.

HOODED WARBLER—*Wilsonia citrina*

PLATE 52

Several male American warblers combine featureless olive upper-parts, clear yellow under-parts, and black on head or throat. In Hooded alone, the black eye is set in the centre of a *large yellow face-patch* (covering forecrown, cheeks and ear-coverts) which in turn is entirely surrounded by black "hood" which extends from top of crown, across side of neck to chin and throat. No wing-bars. Tail in combination with rest of plumage is diagnostic for both sexes at all ages: when closed appears almost uniform with upper-parts, but when widely fanned the *white inner webs* of the three outer tail-feathers (tipped grey-brown) are exposed as three prominent patches on each side, visible for two-thirds of the distance to the tail-coverts from above, and further if viewed from below. Females may show a trace of black bordering the *yellow on head*, but are clear yellow below from bill-base to under-tail coverts. Immatures lack black entirely, with yellow above the eye limited to supercilium which reaches to top of bill; crown and nape olive-green. Legs flesh-coloured. Length about 5½ ins. (14 cms.).

British observers have noted resemblance to a rather green and yellow Melodious Warbler, but with a noticeably long tail, and large, thick, heavy bill very like that of Spotted Flycatcher. Immature Wilson's Warbler (another American not on British list) closely resembles immature Hooded but is smaller and lacks the white tail patches.

It frequents thick under-growth and shrubs in moist deciduous woodland or swampy forest, keeping low down, usually within 10 feet of the ground, but is not normally shy or skulking. Moves actively but rather heavily when feeding in foliage, also regularly makes flycatching sallies. Habitually flicks up and fans its tail, revealing the white patches. Call a metallic "chink".

Status and Distribution. England—One, St. Agnes, Scilly Isles, September 20–23, 1970.

Breeds in eastern U.S.A., and winters in Central America.

SCARLET TANAGER—*Piranga olivacea*

PLATE 53

The breeding male is brilliant *red with black wings and tail*. In autumn and winter the black wings and tail are retained (although acquiring a greenish tinge on feather edges in fresh plumage), while body plumage (blotched with red in early stages of moult) becomes green above, yellowish below, slightly brighter than female. Breeding female's wings and tail are dark greyish-brown (darker than Summer Tanager's). Adult and immature females in autumn resemble autumn female Summer Tanagers but have greenish-olive upper-parts (Summers are browner or more orange), greyish-brown wings (brownish-green in Summers), and lemon-yellow under-parts (Summers dull orange-yellow); under-wing coverts are white (yellow in Summers). Immature male Scarlet Tanagers are similar, but *black on wing-coverts* produces distinctive black patch at carpal joint (Summer Tanagers lack black in all plumages). Bill stout but rather longer than a finch's, slightly smaller and often less pale than Summer Tanager's. See also Summer Tanager. Length about 7¼ ins. (18·5 cms.).

British observers have likened an immature male to Greenfinch without yellow flashes in wings and tail.

A bird of deciduous woodland or well-treed gardens and mature orchards, keeping mainly within the upper foliage where it is more often heard than seen. Note a soft "chip-burr" or "chip-buzz". Takes insects like a large sedate warbler, also fruit in autumn, and sometimes makes agile flycatching sallies.

Status and Distribution. England—Two.

St. Mary's, Scilly Isles, October 4, 1970.

Tresco, Scilly Isles, September 28–October 3, 1975.

Breeds in eastern half of southern Canada and northern and central U.S.A., wintering in South America.

RUFOUS-SIDED TOWHEE—*Pipilo erythrophthalmus*

Plate 54

A distinctive bird, related to buntings. Male is black, with white breast and belly, sharply defined *bright rufous flanks* becoming buffer on under-tail coverts, wings black with white patch near base of primaries and white on outer edge of some flight-feathers, tail black with distal half of outermost pair of feathers white, and less extensive white on distal parts of each of next two pairs. Female has similar pattern but is warm dark brown where male is black. Tail is long, ample and rounded, of shrike-like proportions, and sometimes cocked a little. Eye usually noticeably red. Heavy, finch-like bill. Length about 8 ins. (20 cms.).

Inhabits dense scrubland, untended shrubs, hedge- and bramble-tangles, spending much time on ground; scratches vigorously among dead leaves under bushes, more noisily (although it is smaller and more slender) than our Blackbird. Short-winged; flight usually jerky, low and brief, often showing white spots in outer tail. Not gregarious. Call a loud "chewink".

Status and Distribution. England—One, Lundy Island, Devon, June 7, 1966. (One at Spurn, Yorkshire, September 5,

1975 to January 10, 1976, is widely considered to have had a captive origin).

Breeds in parts of southern Canada, much of U.S.A., and in Mexico. A partial migrant, leaving northern part of range in winter.

FOX SPARROW—*Zonotrichia iliaca*

PLATE 54

One of the largest American buntings, larger than House Sparrow. Sexes similar. In worn plumage (like the bird recorded in Ireland) head and neck are mainly grey, with chestnut cheeks and ear-coverts; mantle olive-brown slightly blotched chestnut, chestnut tones in the wing which has two faint wing-bars, *rump and tail chestnut* and conspicuous in flight. Silvery-white below, heavily streaked with large chestnut-brown markings, which may converge to form a solid patch on centre of breast. In fresh plumage in autumn it is brighter chestnut especially about the head and neck. Length about 7¼ ins. (18·5 cms.).

The short, stout bill of the bird in Ireland gave it the appearance of a bunting, while upper-parts (no doubt ignoring foxy rump and tail colour) suggested a large Dunnock. All observers commented on its slimness; stance very upright.

Wary, frequenting dense woodland undergrowth and edges, tangled thickets, and generally avoiding settlements. Feeds mainly on ground in leaf litter, kicking it aside vigorously. Call a loud "smack" or "stssp"; song is loud, musical and brief.

Status and Distribution. Ireland—One, Copeland, Co. Down, June 3–4, 1961.

Breeds Alaska, much of Canada and west U.S.A., wintering in southern U.S.A.

SONG SPARROW—*Zonotrichia melodia*

PLATE 54

A dull-coloured, streaked American bunting. Crown mainly brownish, with central stripe and supercilium paler and greyer;

darker also on lower border of cheek-patch, and moustache. Mantle is grey-brown, strongly streaked darker; some rufous on wing-coverts; tail rather long, grey-brown, slightly rounded at end, unpatterned. Under-parts whitish, with heavy dark streaks on breast and flanks, coalescing on centre of breast to form an often fairly *conspicuous dark smudge.* Sexes similar. Length about 6¼ ins. (16 cms.).

This is one of several drab, streaked species with rather similar head-patterns. Savannah Sparrow frequents fields and open ground, lacks central smudge on breast, has tail short and notched, forepart of supercilium often yellow; Lincoln's Sparrow has much finer markings on buff band across breast, lower breast and belly unmarked white, narrow white eye-ring.

Most observers of the bird in Britain have noted similarities to Hedge Sparrow, including size, skulking behaviour and drab, streaked upper-parts, but with bill and head-pattern of a bunting.

It frequents low bushy cover, hedges, woodland edges, gardens; preferably near water. Sometimes confiding but more often secretive. Moves tail up and down when perched and in flight. Call a rather nasal "tchenk"; song (which has been heard in England and Scotland) often starts with three similar brisk notes followed by a trill.

Status and Distribution. Britain—Four; all spring records.

Fair Isle, Shetland, April 27—May 10, 1959.

Spurn Point, Yorkshire, May 18, 1964.

Bardsey Island, Caernarvonshire, May 5–8, 1970.

Calf of Man, May 13—June 3, 1971.

Breeds widely in Canada, much of U.S.A. except south-east, and central Mexico. Most leave Canada in winter, spreading through U.S.A. and into Mexico.

WHITE-CROWNED SPARROW—*Zonotrichia leucophrys*

PLATE 55

A handsome American bunting, which may be confused with the browner, less grey, White-throated Sparrow (which see). Adults have upper half of *head striped black and white* (black line through eye and on side of crown, conspicuous white supercilium and centre of crown), clean grey cheeks, neck and breast fading to white on chin; lower flanks brownish; under-parts unstreaked. Back pale grey-brown, broadly striped dark rufous-brown. Two white wing-bars, *bill pink or cinnamon* at all ages. Sexes similar. Immature has similar patterning, but the stripes on head are dark chestnut and buff. Stance is upright; head-shape puffy, erected crown feathers can cause peaking towards rear. Length about 7 ins. (18 cms.).

Outside breeding season it frequents fields and grassy areas, feeding mainly on the ground; much less cover-loving than White-throated.

Status and Distribution. Britain—Two, both in May, 1977.

Fair Isle, Shetland, May 15–16.

Hornsea Mere, Yorkshire, May 22.

Breeds in north and west Canada and west U.S.A. Winters mainly in west and south U.S.A. and west Mexico.

SLATE-COLOURED JUNCO—*Junco hyemalis*

PLATE 55

Unmistakable. A Chaffinch-sized bunting, dark grey and white. Male has unmarked *slate-grey upper-parts*, head, neck, upper breast and flanks (darkest on head); lower breast and belly are pure white, sharply demarcated. *Outer tail-feathers also white*, very conspicuous both in flight and when tail flicked. Bill pale pinkish. Female similar, but duller with some paler brown tinges in the grey; immatures are browner still, especially on flanks, but have same crisp distribution of white as adults. Length about 6¼ ins. (16 cms.).

Unspecialised habitat on passage and in winter: hedges, weedy fields, woodland edges, gardens, bushy places even in towns; not shy. Mainly a ground feeder, but comes readily to bird tables and around farm buildings; often associates with other buntings. Call a light smack or kissing sound "tchick", more twittering in flight; song a modest trill, and a rambling broken subsong of short warbles and twitters.

Status and Distribution. Britain and Ireland—Eight, all in spring.

Loop Head, Co. Clare, May 30, 1905.

Dungeness, Kent, May 26, 1960.

Foula, Shetland, May 1, 1966.

Foula, Shetland, May 10, 1967.

Out Skerries, Shetland, May 7, 1969.

Haresfield, Gloucestershire, April 1–12, 1975.

Bardsey Island, Caernarvonshire, April 25–May 3, 1975.
Loch Affric, Inverness-shire, May 19, 1977.

Breeds across Canada to Alaska and in north-east U.S.A. Winters south-east Canada and most of U.S.A.

CRETZSCHMAR'S BUNTING—*Emberiza caesia*

PLATE 55

It resembles Ortolan Bunting, immatures in particular being very closely similar. Adult male has *blue-grey head and breast* (not greenish grey as Ortolan), *orange* (*not yellow*) *throat*, and rump more rufous. Female is paler than male, with much less evident blue-grey on head and breast; throat is orange-buff, not yellow like female Ortolan's. Immatures tend to have more buffish-chestnut upper-parts than the olive-tinged Ortolan. In all plumages Cretzschmar's have dirty white axillaries and under-wing coverts, while those of Ortolan are pale yellow; both species have pale eye-ring and pinkish bill. It is slightly shorter-winged and more dumpy than Ortolan. Length about 6 ins. (15 cms.).

It breeds in open rocky hill country, often with some scrub, and occurs in marginal cultivation on passage. Rather tame. Feeble song is given from exposed perch on low bush, small tree or rock, usually three syllables "dze dze dzree", often with falling inflection on last note. Call a strong "styip" or incisive "dzip"; alarm "chep".

Status and Distribution. Scotland—One, Fair Isle, Shetland, June 10–20, 1967.

An eastern Mediterranean bird, breeding in Balkans, Cyprus and Turkey south to Israel; winters south to Sudan.

PALLAS'S REED BUNTING—*Emberiza pallasi*

PLATE 56

This account is based largely on information kindly provided by Alan R. Kitson from observations in Mongolia.

A small bunting about the size of Little Bunting, with conspicuous pale rump. Male in spring, with black head and bib and white moustache, recalls male Reed Bunting, but upper-parts are *streaked black and pearl-grey* (not black and brown) almost as contrasting as zebra stripes; *rump is conspicuously whitish*; and hind collar is washed with yellow-orange, becoming white as breeding season advances. Females are normally buffer than female Reed Bunting; they have a more pronounced pair of pale stripes, or "braces", over shoulders and back, and conspicuous *pale buff-white or grey-white rump*. Additional features are more noticeable greyish collar, cheeks without black edging (but often with a black spot in lower, rear corner), fewer streaks (sometimes none) on whitish under-parts. Like Reed Bunting, some chestnut on wing-coverts, and white outer tail-feathers. After autumn moult, the male's new feathers are broadly bordered with buff-ochre, and plumage pattern more resembles that of female: black bib is lost, crown brownish and flecked buff, thin pale supercilium; upper-parts notably buffy, collar and rump pale fawn and ground colour of back pale buff-brown; wing-bars buff, not white, and under-parts tinged buff. Immatures resemble female, but are more brownish-yellow on head. Length about 5¼ ins. (13·5 cms.).

In breeding season occurs in lowlands in river valleys with willow scrub and tussock grass, in steppe, in semi-desert with bushes, also on high plateaux in mountainous areas in bushy tundra or among dwarf birch. On passage normally near ground, in base of willow, tussock grass or reeds, but occasionally found in larger trees. Like Reed Bunting, tail is frequently flicked upwards, with slight fanning which reveals white outer feathers. Calls are "peeseeoo" reminiscent of Yellow-browed Warbler, and "ch-reep" recalling both Tawny Pipit and House Sparrow; both calls are distinct from those of Reed and Little Buntings.

Status and Distribution. Scotland—One, Fair Isle, Shetland, September 29–October 11, 1976.

Breeds central and east Siberia south to Mongolia and N.W. China; migratory, wintering Mongolia, Manchuria south to mid-China.

BOBOLINK—*Dolichonyx oryzivorus*

PLATE 56

A substantial, somewhat bunting-like bird with strong, conical, pointed bill continuing the line of the flat forehead; shows a lot of tawny-yellow in autumn. Male in breeding plumage has *black head and under-parts*, broad tawny-buff patch on nape and back of neck, wings and back mainly black, striped with pale feather edgings, *large whitish scapular patch, and whitish lower back and rump*. Tail black. Female, immatures, and male in autumn are yellowish or buffish below, yellowish-brown above. The striped head pattern is predominent feature, with yellow centre to crown bordered on each side by a broad blackish band, below which is a yellow supercilium and brownish cheek-patch. Upper-parts, wings and flanks are dark-streaked. Tail is unpatterned, and in all plumages each tail-feather tapers to a point. Length about 7¼ ins. (18·5 cms.).

Observers in Britain have noted it as appearing heavier than a Corn Bunting, and the streaked appearance of the upper-parts as resembling Reed Bunting's.

A member of the New World family of Icteridae which includes cowbirds, orioles, grackles. It nests largely in hayfields and in winter normally inhabits open grasslands; on migration it also occurs in rice and corn fields, reeds and other marsh vegetation, feeding mainly on grains and weed-seeds, but may catch insects on the wing. Normal flight strong, without undulation. Migrants call a metallic "pink".

Status and Distribution. Britain and Ireland—Six.

St. Agnes, Scilly Isles, September 19–20, 1962.

St. Mary's, Scilly Isles, October 10, 1968.

Hook Head, Co. Wexford, October 12–14, 1971.

Out Skerries, Shetland, September 18, 1975.

St. Mary's, Scilly Isles, October 9, 1975.

Tresco, Scilly Isles, September 28–29, 1976.

Breeds across south Canada and north U.S.A., and winters in southern half of South America.

INDEX

Following the English names the first figure, in bold type, is the text page number and the second figure is the number of the plate on which the bird is illustrated. The scientific names are followed by the text page numbers only.